REVELATION

In Its Original Meaning

By
Lawrence R. Michaels

Bovee Productions, San Diego, California

I have concluded that the materials presented in this work are free of doctrinal or moral errors.

Bernadeane Carr, STL
Censor Librorum
31 August 2000

In accord with 1983 CIC 827, permission to publish this work is hereby granted.

+ Robert H. Brom
Bishop of San Diego
6 September 2000

Most Scripture texts in this work are taken from <u>The Jerusalem Bible</u>, © 1966, 1967 and 1968 by Doubleday & Company, Inc.

Cover design by Barbara A. Bovee
Published by Bovee Productions
Printed in the United States
ISBN 0-9705295-0-3

TABLE OF CONTENTS

PREFACE

The Book of Revelation can be seen as a writing about a subject with which all Christians are familiar but is most often presented as a subject which is both strange and even foreboding. Any group that identifies itself as Christian could be asked to name the term used to identify the message brought by Jesus to the world and the group would easily answer that the term is "Gospel." Asked further for the name of the person who identified Jesus as the one sent by God with the message and they would respond just as easily that it was "John the Baptist." The first verse of the Book of Revelation provides the same answers with almost the same clarity so long as any Christian group isn't told the source of that first verse. Everyone should expect that "Gospel" and an introduction of Jesus Christ would be present in some form in a book that is part of the New Testament. What else is the New Testament about?

Yet, it might be equally true that if any such group of Christians were to read that first verse, after being told that it came from the Book of Revelation, they would respond with a combination of silence, blank stares, confusion and a number of contradictory explanations. The contradictory explanations would most likely suggest a late first century context involving a Roman persecution of Christians and, probably, a future return of Jesus to set up some type of kingdom. All of the group members might give some assent to such a proposal. Yet, everyone might also admit that there is no distinct understanding of such a conclusion in the rest of the New Testament except this so-called last book. Those proposing a 1000-year period for such a kingdom would make little effort to explain the nearly 2000-year period already past while waiting for the result. Jesus mentioned to his disciples that some of them would not "taste death before they see the kingdom of God come with power" (Mk 9:1). Since "taste" must mean the experience of natural death, we might wonder if any of the group would suggest Jesus Christ was wrong or might they question if the basis for most interpretations of the Book of Revelation are "off the mark" if

2

not completely wrong.

The Book of Revelation is composed almost entirely from quotations and allusions derived from the Old Testament. The great descriptions of Jesus Christ, his specific teachings, his great miracles and the writings of his disciples are absent and, seemingly, unknown in this so-called last book of the New Testament. The Book contains descriptions which are interpreted as referring to Jesus Christ even though they are quite different from New Testament terms for Jesus. This discrepancy would not be unacceptable for a very early writing about the coming of Jesus Christ but such a solution is rarely suggested and, perhaps, even more rarely accepted.

This commentary starts with what all Christians know about the first century and what would be known by those who originally waited for a Messiah. If the Book seems to be a record of a vision, as it tells us that it is, that will be accepted. If the Book is an early first century writing, it is quite possible that the coming of Jesus Christ already has happened and that too will be accepted. In short, this commentary is intended to examine what all Christians know about the coming of Jesus Christ that did occur. It is the story of a great success that, without almost 2000 years of waiting and speculation, has resulted in nearly two billion people on earth today being called Christian. Its conclusion is not a question of waiting for yet another 1000 years for Jesus to tell us about "things that are now to take place very soon," but to celebrate again what did take place when he came "very soon" just as he had promised. It's a commentary about a book on a Revelation that revealed in the first century what was so important to know in the first century.

This book, like all books, is not the work of only the individual whose name is noted on the cover. The support of many was necessary to make this book possible, and I am thankful for those who provided that important element, and yet, I have added a few names in special recognition and appreciation. First and foremost, in special thanks to Our Lord, Jesus Christ, for the unending opportunities for me to find the time, and have the talent and patience to produce this material. Likewise, a special thank you to my wife, Jean, for her endless hours of work and support and her unending patience which I often stretched further than should have been necessary. A special thanks and appreciation to Richard Bohen, a dear friend and confidant, for his many hours of expertise in publishing and for reviewing the copy. His and his wife Kay's support started with my first involvement in bible studies and has been continuous through all these endeavors. Thanks especially to Barbara and Michael Bovee for their professional help in producing this work. Starting the project was my decision, but bringing it to completion through all the difficulties of publishing was their essential gift. I wish to thank Bernadeane Carr who in her review for errors also provided a great many comments which improved the text and added clarity for the readers. Finally, a great thanks to the many who have patiently sat through these presentations in classes in the diocesan programs and in the parishes where they have been offered. They may have thought they were receiving a gift while in reality they were providing a reflection which added to the final product.

INTRODUCTION

The Book of Revelation is the mystery writing of the New Testament. It has a message with a glorious conclusion and comes with a sense of urgency, but has been difficult to explain or even place in time. Quoted more often than any other New Testament writing in the second century, it later had opposition to being included in the New Testament canon when that was defined at the end of the fourth century. Placed at the end of the New Testament, it often is seen as the last writing of Scripture even though there is little evidence to support such a conclusion. Any reading of the Book shows it to be heavily dependent on Old Testament quotations with almost no connections to the New Testament. Except for the first nine verses and the last six verses, Revelation has very few direct references to Christianity as described in the New Testament.

Yet, the opening verses of the Book give a very different view from being the last book of the New Testament or one related to the unproven theories underlying nearly all commentaries on its contents. The readers are simply told in the first verse that it is a revelation given by God to Jesus Christ so he could tell his servants about what is to take place "very soon." It also mentions that John was told about the Revelation by an angel (messenger) and has written down "everything he saw" which seems to be the visions in the Book. After more than 1,900 years everyone could conclude that what has come through Jesus Christ, what was accepted by his disciples, and what has been known from the first century might be that revelation. Likewise, John the Baptist preceded Jesus and told of his coming "very soon" and what we have in writing may be his own writing. However, even though all Christians understand what happened at that time from the other 26 books of the New Testament, there is a great reluctance to make the tie of that historical record to this Book.

This commentary is an attempt to make clear what should be known by all Christians. John came as a prophet to introduce Jesus as the Messiah (Christ) so that his disciples would believe his message was from God, including its conclusion that Jesus is God incarnated. As such, the Book is a truly great introduction to the remainder of Jesus' revelation included in the teachings of the church founded by Jesus and the other 26 books of the New Testament. This commentary is not a new understanding but the one accepted at the start of Jesus' public life, as we would expect.

The chief characteristic of the Book is a method of writing that has become known as apocalyptic. The term is derived from the opening statement of the Book that it is an apocalypse, a Greek word which means revelation and hence the name of the Book. However, while the New Testament is very much a record of the revelation of Jesus Christ, the Book of Revelation often is seen as its most difficult book to understand and, from a practical standpoint, would be the least revelatory of its content. Certainly, in relation to its length, it is the least used of the major books of the New Testament. Recent attempts to redefine apocalyptic writing as a literary form common in Jewish/Christian circles from 200 BC to 100 AD may have been important in classifying a number of intertestamental writings which were not accepted as Scripture. However, contrary to any claim by those who support the redefinition, it did nothing to clarify the Book of Revelation and may have been a means to legitimize its apparent difficulties.

The major problems with Revelation seem to arise from the context selected for its interpretation. The end of the first century AD in a time of persecution in Asia Minor is accepted as the context of the writing almost universally. Even Christian groups who use Scripture in the most literalistic way, often with no concern for using the context to determine the meaning of other books of Scripture, adhere to that late context for its interpretation. While a knowledge of context is necessary for understanding any writing, if a chosen context produces only confusion, it would be reasonable to reexamine the context selection. With Revelation such difficulties are swept aside on the basis that apocalyptic writing is often in a type of code where the words could easily have a very different or even opposite meaning from what is literal. The result is an explanation which often is exceedingly difficult to understand and rarely produces wide acceptance in different faith communities or by the Christian public as a whole. The fact that a writing that is called Revelation actually seems to hide any clear meaning is hardly considered to be a problem.

An examination of the Book even on a superficial level shows that it is a description of some visions or of a single vision with a number of scenes. In the opening verses the visions are said to be from God and the later descriptions bear out that conclusion. There is an urgency noted at the start and finish that what is seen in the visions should become known on earth through the prophet John who is the sole witness to the visions. However, there are no actions described in the Book other than the directions given to John to write down what he sees. Also, in most commentaries, there are few real connections to anything in the first century since the visions seem to be about the whole plan of God from the start of creation to its end point in a last judgment. Therefore, the context of when the visions were given cannot be determined from the vision itself, even though clues can be found in a comparison of terms from the other New Testament writings and Revelation.

The writing of the Book includes some statements which are used by interpreters to justify the context at the end of the first century. However, even those statements do not agree with that late first century context since what is described seems to occur prior to the destruction of the Jerusalem temple in the year 70. Commentators often place the time of the writing as occurring after what is shown in the vision, as future events, have taken place. The vision then would be seen as something invented by the author to give the impression that the message is truly from heaven. Other commentators assume that the writing is a combination of two or more visions which incorporate several events from different time frames in order to have a finished product at the end of the first century while including earlier predictions of events.

The purpose and goal of this commentary is to examine

the Book of Revelation with respect to a context that is found in it and which also fits with the development of the New Testament. It is an examination that is intended to follow the instructions of the Pontifical Biblical Commission for teaching Scripture in the Church[1] that requires an examination of context for any writing in the Bible. Where the Book of Revelation fits into a time line of the New Testament should relate to what it says to that part of the first century development of Christianity. The finding of a true context would be as important as the commentary itself and, certainly, is the initial effort for any commentary. Yet, the proof of a correct context is what the Book then says to the early church and allows present day Christians to apply that inspired meaning to their own situations.

In reading this background section and the commentary that follows, it should be noted that all dates are AD unless noted. All Scripture references without a book name, but only with a chapter and verse designation, are taken from the Book of Revelation. While this background section is intended to make it easier to understand the commentary section, it will turn out for most readers that the opposite also is true. What is presented as a basis for making the commentary clear will become clearer itself if reread after finishing the commentary. For many readers this exercise will be closer to being introduced to a new book of Scripture than a reintroduction to a familiar one.

APOCALYPTIC LITERATURE

Apocalyptic writing has been noted in Scripture since before the time of Christ and in this New Testament book, since the second century. However, a proposal that there is a type of literature that can be defined as apocalyptic has a far more limited history starting in the 19th century, but has been subject to particular scrutiny in the last half of the 20th century. The term arises primarily from the Book of Revelation, yet has been defined to include other Old Testament and intertestamental writings that have some similarities to Revelation. Initially the primary similarity among the writings was a language that used symbolism and numbers that could only be understood by readers

8

with a special knowledge of such symbolism rather than a general readership at large. Interpretation of such writing included a decoding of hidden meanings to gain the needed insights to fully understand the text. That approach worked quite well with the book of Daniel since the context was known to be in the period that caused the Maccabee's revolt in 167-164 BC.

In time, other features of such writing were suggested which tended to open the category of literature to a wider collection of books. That process resulted in a redefinition of apocalyptic literature in the nineteen seventies based on a wide review and study of such literature. The result of the work was a definition that stated: "Apocalypse is a genre of revelatory literature with a narrative framework, in which a revelation is mediated by an otherworldly being to a human recipient, disclosing a transcendent reality which is both temporal, insofar as it envisages eschatological salvation, and spatial, insofar as it involves another, supernatural world."[2]

Such a definition starts from the assumption that such a form of literature exists and that a great many examples are available in literature from many sources. The definition is a bridging of similarities between all the examples selected, probably with less attention paid to how such examples exhibit differences that would argue against such a form. The publication of the definition brought about a number of suggestions which would tend to expand the definition. The expansion provided further assurances that such a type of literature exists on a far greater scale than might have been imagined at the outset.

It should be noted that such an exercise is based, at least partly, on how the primary examples of such literature are interpreted, and, certainly, the Book of Revelation is the prize example. As a result, any attempt to examine a new understanding of Revelation must go far beyond a simple toppling of earlier understandings; it must challenge the whole basis for a new definition of apocalyptic literature. Yet, Revelation as interpreted, to some extent at least, by those developing and later reviewing the new definition, does not fit the context of the first century for Christianity nor does the new definition necessarily fit the actual text of Revelation itself. That doesn't mean that a form of literature described as apocalyptic doesn't exist, but it could change its application to Revelation. The definition of this Book as apocalyptic based on criteria only developed some nineteen centuries after it was written establishes an understanding which may not have been the intent of the author. If the author's intent was otherwise, then surely that intent would be completely obliterated by such an assumption.

Even the characteristics of definitions of apocalyptic literature earlier than the 1986 attempt have never fit Revelation very easily except in the mind of the translator. Pseudonymity of the author is a recognized common trait of such literature, yet in Revelation the name of the author is clearly given even if not recognized very often by commentators. Moreover, the way the name is given indicates that the reader would recognize the person. Apocalyptic writing usually proposes a great catastrophe, but in Revelation such an event must be read into the text, otherwise the narration of the vision is entirely about the plan of God for all of creation. Evil power associated with political power and in opposition to God's rule would be common to earlier definitions and that could be seen in Revelation. However, much of what might be seen as evil power in Revelation is little more than empires and kingdoms that worship pagan idols rather than the True God. That condition represented the situation of the world outside of Judaism and Christianity in the first century. Symbolic language is often seen as a characteristic of apocalyptic writing, yet the highly symbolic language which is common in Revelation is derived from Old Testament quotations more than from the form of literature. Finally, an eschatological orientation which is found in such writing could be seen as common to most of the New Testament. The coming of the "King of Kings" and his victory are not an end time episode but something occurring an indefinitely long time (1,000 years) before the eschatological event. The last judgment is given as the disappearance of creation followed by a process to determine who chose a disappearing earth as their life and who chose eternal heaven (20:12). So, if these are the more common characteristics of apocalyptic literature, they don't show up too clearly in Revelation unless the commentator decides to find them there.

Clearly the author of Revelation has borrowed heavily from the Old Testament. One reason to do that was to explain the meaning of the visions in a way that would show God's intention to save the world and also could be recognized by the Jewish people and Jewish Christian people. Anything which could not be seen as the work of Yahweh and, therefore, consistent with the Old Testament record of revelation would hardly be accepted by such people. The preaching of apostles could be seen as being the same type of borrowing from the Old Testament, especially in presentations to the synagogues as seen often in Paul's preaching. Those apostles were attempting to show Jewish people that the Old Testament is fulfilled through the acceptance of Jesus as the Messiah (Acts 28:23-25).

Revelation would be the same type of exercise using that which was understood clearly from the Old Testament rather than being an attempt to hide the revelation in a code that only a few could understand. The context of a vision of the coming of a saving Messiah prior to the public life of Jesus which makes clear the message from the Old Testament would be a most important aspect. At that date, the apocalyptic intertestamental literature may not have been known by the author of Revelation, let alone be used as a model. Ruling that Revelation is apocalyptic under the new definition may actually destroy any attempt to determine the true message.

The definition of apocalyptic literature could include almost all of Scripture when apocalyptic literature is defined in terms such as: revelatory literature, narrative, mediated by other-worldly beings to humans, about a transcendent reality, involving salvation and a supernatural world. This is a description of the clearest parts of all of Scripture. Certainly the teachings of Jesus would almost entirely fit that description. When a definition is overly broad, it doesn't define anything.

One obvious characteristic of apocalyptic writing in the Old Testament is the use of language that seems to hide the identity of the author and obscure the meaning of the message to outsiders. Often seen as a type of code are the bizarre images and often incomprehensible descriptions which are used in such texts. Only those who could understand the hidden meanings of such things would ever come to know the revelation which was presented.

This partial hiding of a message meant to be revealed is seen in the Old Testament writings where the writer's life could be endangered if his identity became known. Ezekiel wrote to the first group of exiles in Babylon in what is sometimes a message of hope, which could be considered seditionary if read and understood by their captors. His description of the chariot of Yahweh (Ez 1:4-28) must have meant that the people in exile could have contact with Yahweh even while being separated from the Holy Land. Yahweh could travel throughout the heavens at high speeds and without the need to slow down even for turns and so could always hear their prayers. Yet the description would not be clear to anyone who didn't recognize how important that meaning would be to the Israelites.

Second Isaiah may have written more clearly about the Israelites future return to the Holy Land but if the author added his message to the Isaiah scroll without any other identification, it would look like a writing of more than a century before the exile. The meaning would become clear only to one who knew where the original Isaiah scroll ended. We don't know with any real certainty if Second Isaiah was added to the Isaiah scroll while the Jews were in captivity in Babylon. The collection of texts into the final scrolls must have continued after the return to Jerusalem which would make unclear the basis for adding Second and, later, Third Isaiah to an earlier scroll. However, anyone writing such a hopeful statement of divine help would have been interested in hiding the exilic writings from their captors.

Daniel was written during the time of the Maccabean revolt with a message of hope that was meant to be widely read at that time. To camouflage his message, he back dated it by reference to the time of the exile, used the name of a historical figure as the author and used coded language. With such measures, he essentially created major features of the apocalyptic format.

However, it became a message of great hope once it could be tied to the time of the Maccabees.

The Christian message is never meant to be hidden or obscured. Jesus tells his disciples to "uncover what is covered, make clear what is hidden" (Lk 12:2), and what has been whispered should be proclaimed from the rooftops (Lk 12:3). One thrust of Mark's Gospel is that even during the persecution of Nero, Christians should have witnessed to the Romans about the message of Christ. The result may have been death for those disciples but that witness reflects the same as the witness on the cross in terms of building the kingdom (Mk 4:21-29). Surely the urgency of the message given to John in Revelation (1:1 and 22:6-10) indicates it should be made known very clearly. Therefore, the hidden meaning that may have been necessary for Ezekiel, Second Isaiah and Daniel is not appropriate for a Christian writing in Scripture, nor can that be proposed as the intent of the directions given to John.

A question could even be raised about Revelation even being apocalyptic writing even though it was from Revelation (Apocalypse in Greek) that such writing gained its name. Much of the imagery that causes Revelation to be called apocalyptic is not in the actual writing of the Book itself. The great number of quotations from apocalyptic-style verses in the Old Testament are behind much of that imagery. John seems to use such quotations to show specifically that the meaning of the images seen in this vision comes from the Old Testament. He could just describe the beast from the sea as seen in the vision (13:1) but the description includes the references to leopard, bear and lion (13:2) to equate the beast to the beasts of Daniel (Dan 7:1-6) at least in terms of the political power behind an empire. The quotations make the meaning far more clear to anyone familiar with the Old Testament than would any new description written by John without such connections. The same could be said for many of the other images in Revelation.

The Old Testament apocalyptic writings were intended to propose a time for the coming of a Messiah or a final stable period of independence for Israel under God. John, as the author of Revelation, would quote them when the conditions described in them are about to be fulfilled according to John's interpretation of the vision. While the original material may have had a hidden meaning, in this Book the quotations are a means of explaining quite openly what is to come "soon." Just as Christians mined the Old Testament for quotes that could be interpreted as messianic and seemed to be fulfilled in Jesus Christ, so the witness to the vision seems to do the same.

Making ties to the Old Testament, or describing everything in reference to the Old Testament, would assure the readers that the visions are from God, rather than just a meaningless story. Therefore, it is reasonable to question if Revelation is an apocalyptic writing. This is especially true if it produces someone like John the Baptist who in this commentary is seen as the author and who dedicates his life to making the message known and is widely accepted as a prophet. The prophecy from the vision tells of a change coming upon the people of Israel which incorporates their entire religious background and, except for the judgment after the "1,000 years," will happen during their lifetime. Only the last two chapters contain an end time presentation; everything else is a plan of God already partly known from Israel's history and with this writing answers fully the questions that Judaism attempted to answer through the wisdom literature.

Therefore, the modern designation of Revelation in terms of a newly-revised definition of apocalyptic literature may interfere with its interpretation more than it helps in finding the true meaning. If this Book is meant to be a very clear revelation of a message from God, at a time when God took on a human nature and personally proclaimed the message to the people most prepared to receive it, present day Christians should see the message clearly. When there are great divisions in how different Christian groups interpret the Book, and none of them are overly clear, the question should be at least raised, should we be looking for a clearer interpretation?

CONTEXT OF REVELATION

NEW TESTAMENT CONTEXT

The context of the church in the first century is one which reflects a great change in understanding the relationship with God. However, the starting point for that change is about four centuries earlier when a Jewish understanding developed of Yahweh being the only God of all creation. That view originated sometime after the Exile, but resulted from the Exile and the search for understanding of the reasons behind that event. The wisdom literature of the Old Testament became the vehicle for Jewish speculation about how the covenant based on the Law could relate to this unique understanding of God, unknown by any other people.

The reassurance that came to Judaism from the wisdom literature promoted a rigid keeping of the Law yet opened up concepts that had never been a clear part of the Law. A belief in an afterlife came to be accepted without being completely defined. A living of the covenant relationship by all Jews was promoted by Pharisees in the synagogues following traditions of the elders which went beyond the Law. A rising expectation of the coming of the Messiah must have been present with the loosening of foreign control in Palestine and the rebuilding of the temple. All of these developments provided a conditioning of Jewish thought beyond the literal interpretations of the writings of the Law and Prophets by the early first century.

The New Testament period could be defined as the period starting with the public life of Jesus in about 27 and continuing until the last writings of the New Testament near the end of the century. Jesus' birth and some early events would precede that period while the earliest writings of a New Testament document would be mid-century and the earliest attempts to determine a canon of the writings would be near the middle of the second century. The context of events and writings are shown in the following chart, titled New Testament Time Line, and with the unfolding of those events and writings, an expansion of

NEW TESTAMENT TIME LINE

30 A.D.	The Resurrection of Jesus Christ	
	Stephen Martyred	
	Paul's Conversion	
40 A.D.	Cornelius	
	Paul's First Journey	
	Council of Jerusalem	
50 A.D.	Paul's Second Journey	1 & 2 Thessalonians
		Philippians
	Paul's Third Journey	1 & 2 Corinthians
		Galatians
		Romans
	Paul in Caesarea	
60 A.D.	Paul in Rome	James
		Ephesians, Colossians
		Philemon
	Nero's Persecution 64-68	1 Peter
	Peter & Paul Martyred	1 & 2 Timothy/Titus
	Jewish Revolt 66-70	
		GOSPEL OF MARK
70 A.D.	Temple Destroyed	
		Hebrews
	Council	
80 A.D.	of	GOSPEL OF MATTHEW
		Jude
	Jamnia	
		GOSPEL OF LUKE
		Acts of Apostles
90 A.D.	Separation from Judaism	GOSPEL OF JOHN
		1, 2, 3 John
	Domitian's Persecution 95-96	Revelation
		2 Peter
100 A.D.		

understanding occurred among disciples of the early church.

While the general dating of the writings are widely accepted, many of the writings have little real justification for their placement. Paul's writings in the 50s have very strong support for their positions usually within a variation of only a year or two between the estimates of the great majority of scholars. Mark's Gospel is strongly supported as the earliest of the Gospels, and as resulting from the effect of Nero's persecution, even through some prominent scholars would propose other solutions. Matthew and Luke are widely accepted as being produced through additions to Mark's Gospel and yet with a dating sufficiently close to each other as to be independent additions. However, even with that agreement, the actual dates for those two Gospels have very little solid support or any definitive justification. John's Gospel is considered to be the last of the four, but the actual date is unclear. The other writings have less basis for suggesting a specific date and the variation of dates reflects the unsubstantiated opinion of each scholar with little outside support.

The Judaism of the time of Jesus had changed in the previous three centuries, and it was changing both in Palestine and the diaspora at the time of Jesus. It would be subjected to greater change both from the revelation brought by the Messiah and the destruction of the temple in 70. The coming of John the Baptist as a prophet and Jesus as the Messiah was accompanied by a call for a change which is defined as repentance or reform. For Judaism, repenting could have been interpreted as a step toward personal holiness by all Jews that was required prior to entering into a permanent kingdom of God on earth, governed by the Messiah. It would be a fulfillment of the promise made to David and echoed by prophets and known as the Day of the Lord. The result would be a great afterlife reward for those judged worthy but with a strong indication of a terrible punishment for those judged unworthy. Baptism by John the Baptist seemed to offer a special opportunity to declare oneself in support of the kingdom and show a determination to make the change necessary to be accepted. The Pharisee group within Judaism had already suggested that everyone should put themselves under the directives of the Law (often more related to the priests and temple functions than to the individual lives of Jews) through a rigid following of the traditions of the Elders.

The coming of Jesus as the Messiah supported such an expectation even though he didn't exactly support the Pharisees' teachings, at least to their satisfaction. This description of the kingdom may not have been clear to the people with a very different expectation. His teaching on repenting went somewhat beyond the actual wording of the Law and the traditions of the Elders which were intended to apply the Law to the everyday life of the people. However, even the disciples of Jesus seem to follow their initial inclination on what a Messiah would mean in Judaism rather than focusing on what might seem like inconsistencies between Jesus' teachings and those historical traditions. While the Resurrection of Jesus would point toward a relationship beyond the Law, and was used that way by the early church, the disciples even at the Ascension were asking about the restoring of the "kingdom to Israel" (Acts 1:6).

The persistence of this view of the Messiah resulted in an expectation among Jesus' disciples of an early second coming of Jesus to make their view of the kingdom a reality. The expectation of the early return produced an emphasis on a continuation of Jesus' ministry by the disciples within Judaism. The initial intent was to cause an acceptance of the Messiah within Judaism as the earthly leader of the kingdom even as David had been seen as the earthly agent of Yahweh their true king. The acceptance would result in a covenant relationship that went beyond the covenant created under the Law and, yet, might be quite easily seen as its fulfillment. That meaning would have become known in essentially every synagogue in the world through pilgrims coming to Jerusalem and hearing about Jesus' public life, and especially of the Passover and Pentecost events related to Jesus' death and resurrection, and repeated on returning to their home synagogues. Such stories would be very important to the synagogues since the expectation in Jerusalem on that fateful Passover was that Jesus was the Messiah. The on-going preaching activity by the disciples on the temple mount after the Resurrection, along with the growth in the number who had accepted that teaching, would have continued to expand the stories known about Jesus in synagogues world-wide. The simplicity of the expected response, to accept baptism and faithfully live the meaning of the Law until the second coming, would be combined with an urgency for everyone to make the decision prior to the second coming. Such pressure for an early baptism decision would have assured growth of the sect within Judaism.

The start of a change in the context of the early church occurred as the promise of a place in the expected kingdom was opened first to Samaritans (Acts 8:4-70) within a few years after the Resurrection. Peter and John confirmed such a practice quite easily, perhaps as a result of Jesus' earlier preaching among Samaritans (Jn 4:1-42). However, a similar opening to Gentiles (Acts 10:1-48) was not well accepted even by Peter who was involved in it (Acts 11:1-18). Peter seems to have treated that episode as an exception to the true meaning of the kingdom. Only Paul's later experience of baptizing Gentiles on his first journey raised the real question of how Gentiles could be accepted into the kingdom (Acts 14:21-28) and caused the apostolic church to officially approve such a change (Acts 15:1-35). Judaism would not allow an integration of Jews and Gentiles so the division between official Judaism and Jews who accepted the Messiah could be identified in a clash of doctrines.

Many or even most Jews would refuse to become part of such radical departure from the traditions of great separation from Gentiles prevalent since the return from the exile. The success among Christians in an opening to Gentile converts must have been accompanied by resistance by Jews to becoming new converts to what was becoming a separate Christian religion. The actual severing of relations between Jews and Christians usually is proposed as an action by Judaism at the Council of Jamnia (c. 70-90). However, the practical separation might have started much earlier as Christians seem to establish their own synagogues rather than attending synagogues of mixed

Jews and Jewish Christians (Acts 14:23) and shown on a larger scale when Paul reached Rome in 61 (Acts 28:22). A decree of the Council of Jamnia required a petition to be included in a synagogue prayer asking God to "curse the deviators," meaning the Christians.[3] That decree probably extended the separation to Jewish Christians, in addition to Gentile Christians, still part of Jewish synagogues as in the period immediately after the Resurrection, and made the separation complete.

The final stage of change for the developing Christian covenant understanding would have occurred after the separation from Judaism as the Gospel of John was circulated showing that Jesus' own words indicated that the full message was that He is divine. More than just a virgin birth through an action of God, Jesus applies the Yahweh name from the Old Testament to himself (Jn 8:58). Once that occurred the Revelation had been completed. The early concept of a second coming by Jesus to establish a kingdom on earth had been shown to be a misunderstanding in Mark's Gospel by a simple review of Jesus' own words (Mk 13:1-27). When the sun and moon are darkened and the stars fall from the sky, when creation ends, there would be a second coming as a last judgment. Luke in his Gospel had emphasized the need to be conscientious disciples forming the kingdom rather than just waiting for a return. The divinity understanding in John's Gospel made an early second coming to produce a kingdom on earth absolutely meaningless as shown by experience up to that time.

Therefore, there are some rather dramatic changes in Christian understanding in the first century which can be used for dating and understanding the writings. A second coming by Jesus to set up a kingdom on earth can be seen in the writings related to the time of the Ascension and perhaps they persisted for two decades afterward. Paul addressed the subject in his first letter to the Thessalonians (1 Thes 4:13-18) but even there it has the appearance of a final judgment. Chapter 13 of Mark's Gospel reviews the return of Jesus much more completely and establishes that the second coming only has a last judgment meaning. So the end point is clear by the year 70 and may have been settled earlier but then brought back for discussion in Mark's time only by the horrors of Nero's persecution.

The separation of Christianity from Judaism had its starting point before the destruction of the temple in 70, and the final stages are less well defined. The theory that the Council of Jamnia may have continued until 80 or 90 before making a decision on the separation from Christianity fits a late date for the completion of the New Testament writings. Yet the evidence in the last chapter of Acts indicates the decision to separate was completed as a practical matter even before the temple was destroyed. In addition, there is little reason to believe that the formal decision at Jamnia would have been difficult to make or delayed long once Judaism contemplated what might have caused the loss of God's protection for Jerusalem and the temple. The destruction of the temple at the time of the Babylonian exile seems to have been blamed on connections to Gentile religions through the use of Canaanite altars on high places for sacrifices (2 Kgs 23:4, 13-14, 26-27). A major change had occurred in the first century by allowing Gentiles to become Christian without first becoming Jewish and, therefore, the separation from Christianity would have seemed necessary for Judaism to reestablish a separation from Gentiles.

Once a question arises about the late date of Revelation by suggesting that it must be prior to the destruction of the temple, the chronology of the writing of the Gospels and later New Testament writings also is subject to change. Mark's Gospel seems to be written after the persecution of Nero ended in 68 and before the temple was destroyed in 70. Matthew's Gospel seems addressed to the questions of Christianity being separated from Judaism and Luke's Gospel to a separation already affecting his community. However, both follow Mark and, yet, are written close enough together that neither Matthew nor Luke are aware of each other's work. The dating of these two is often stretched out over two decades after Mark's Gospel but without any real evidence or basis in fact.

Mark's Gospel could have been available to the communities of Matthew and Luke within a year after it was written and the separation question relating to Matthew and Luke was already in existence in Rome before Nero's persecution. Separation could have been addressed by adding teachings and sayings of Jesus to Mark's Gospel by Matthew and Luke within a few years after 70. John's Gospel, if triggered by the circulation of a translation of Revelation into Greek for distribution outside of Palestine, as is raised in the epilogue of this commentary, could have been written in the decade of the 70s rather than a decade or two later. The dating of the New Testament writings other than Paul's early letters is not so solidly based on evidence that it withstands the effect of a change in the dating of Revelation. The concept of a dating of Revelation at the end of Domitian's reign in 95-96 is based on assumptions, but in fact, could have hidden real evidence for an earlier dating of the Gospels and a closing of the New Testament period.

As stated earlier, finding a meaning for any writing of Scripture requires an understanding of the context of its writing. The meaning of Scripture can never come in what a later reader declares it to mean in the reader's own life without destroying the meaning of inspiration. The writer is the one inspired to produce the word of God in human language. To find the meaning of the writing, it is necessary to determine what the writer was attempting to convey, in human language, about the inspiration that came from God. The context of the writing is an essential element to determine what the writer was attempting to proclaim in the situation of that writing or, more clearly, in its context.

TRADITIONAL CONTEXT OF REVELATION

The commonly accepted context of the Book of Revelation comes from traditions that can be traced back to the end of the second century. Even though there are arguments to the contrary on one issue or another, the context can be stated as follows:

1. Written in 95-96 in response to Domitian's persecution or in anticipation of it,
2. Subject is a second coming to establish a 1,000-year

reign or to establish a reign after the 1,000-year period,

3. Author is John the Evangelist or someone from the Johannine community,

4. Place of writing is Asia Minor and probably Ephesus,

5. Literary form is apocalyptic writing.

The date selected for the writing is not based on anything in the Book directly, but on the occasion of the first persecution in Asia Minor during the last two years of the reign of the Emperor Domitian. There is little evidence in the Book for a persecution. Perhaps the use of the Greek word martus, translated as martyr, tends to suggest persecution. However, martus simply means witness and only late in the second century did it gain the meaning of someone who died for holding firm to their Christian faith. That would be an exceedingly strong witness and, therefore, would become the description of the perfect witness, but would not be used in that way in a first-century writing.

The concept of a second coming by Jesus Christ to set up a kingdom on earth was an early Christian expectation. However, even in the earliest writings, Paul addresses the subject as an event not on earth (1 Thes 4:13-18) and even includes some last judgment allusions (II Thes 1:8-9). The church's understanding of the "one thousand year reign" had by the fifth century become the present time after the Resurrection and prior to the second coming in a last judgment. A literal 1,000-year reign starting with a return of Jesus Christ has been adopted by some fundamentalist groups starting in the 19th century.

A connection between Revelation and the community of John the Evangelist was included in the earliest traditions about the Book and is examined in the epilogue of this commentary. However, a major reason for the early resistance of the Eastern Churches to accepting this Book into the New Testament canon was the certainty that the author of the Fourth Gospel could not have been the author of Revelation. The dramatic difference in the Greek writing between the two books seemed to rule out such a connection. It would be equally reasonable to believe that such differences would not occur within writings originating from that community even if John the Evangelist were the authority behind the writings, but not the actual scribe. There could be no justification for such incredibly poor Greek to be used in that community for Revelation after having prepared the Fourth Gospel in correct Greek even though written with a limited vocabulary.

The place of the writing is an early tradition, but it most likely is derived from the text itself in the mention of the seven cities of Asia Minor. Certainly the letters themselves would seem to have been written for that area if they are additions to the rest of the Book. The connections to John's Gospel, which has traditions of being written in Ephesus, are used as an argument for Revelation coming from the same area. However, the traditions of John's Gospel being written in Ephesus are sometimes based on its parallels with Revelation, in which case, the connection would be an example of circular reasoning.

The designation of Revelation as apocalyptic writing is discussed earlier under that subject. The text certainly includes some apocalyptic characteristics, but much of it is included in the quotations and allusions taken from the Old Testament. However, there are a few places where such language is used in Revelation which cannot be attributed to outside sources. The difficulty in applying such a designation is that even the Gospels fulfill parts of the new definition of apocalyptic writing in that the message "envisages eschatological salvation" and "involves another, supernatural world." Certainly Jesus is "an otherworldly being" mediating revelation to a human recipient. Once the definition was changed to include enough writings to justify the designation of apocalyptic literature, it includes so much literature that its uniqueness disappears.

EARLY CONTEXT OF REVELATION

The traditional context for the Book of Revelation has no support in the first century or the early second century even though the Book is quoted very often during the second century. The earliest tradition about the reign of Domitian is from Ireaneus near the end of the second century. There are some traditions that place the writing of Revelation in the reign of Emperor Claudius (41-54) or Nero (54-68), but they are unsubstantiated by anything other than the quotations from the fourth century or later.

Present day support for an early context for Revelation was developed by Josephine Ford of the University of Notre Dame in the Anchor Bible book Revelation.[4] Her conclusion comes from examining the Book itself to look for internal clues to the context in a way not duplicated by any other scholar. The lack of New Testament connections in the Book and, especially, the lack of almost any mention of Jesus in chapters four to eleven, along with the overwhelming number of Old Testament quotations, support her assumption that the context could be early.

The relationship between "Lamb of God," the "bridegroom," "He that comes," and "baptism by fire" in Revelation[5] and the sections concerning John the Baptist in the Gospels support her contention that John the Baptist was the author or source behind at least chapters four to eleven. "Lamb" and the Messiah as "bridegroom" are found only in Revelation and in the sections of the Fourth Gospel where John the Baptist is speaking (Jn 1:29-34 and Jn 3:28-29), pointing to the direct connection between John the Baptist and the John of Revelation. "He that comes" and "baptism by fire" might not be quite as dramatic but the same closeness is evident and John the Baptist's anger at the Pharisees and Sadducees (Mt 3:7-12) may express the condemnation of temple worship found in Revelation. Ford placed chapters 12 to 22 at a later time because the name of Jesus is used, but still considers it a writing coming from the disciples of John the Baptist and earlier than the writing of the Gospels. Even that lateness seems to be more related to the last two or three chapters of the Book than to chapters 12 to 19.[6]

The first three chapters are attributed by Ford to a Christian writer who may have originally been a disciple of John the Baptist.[7] The Christian designation was based on what is described as "clear Christological characteristics" in these chapters. These chapters, along with parts of the last six verses of chapter 22, would have been written after 60 and, in her view, stress an "imminent second coming."[8]

A second writing that promotes an early context comes from another Catholic scholar, Eugenio Corsini from the University of Turin, Italy, in his book The Apocalypse.[9] While his approach does not break the Book into sections written at different times, as does Josephine Ford, he clearly identifies Revelation as a prophecy announcing the original coming of Jesus Christ. So his interpretation of the meaning speaks to the same context as Ford, even if it comes from a different type of argument.

Once the context of John the Baptist is examined, a great many changes in understanding can be seen in the text which often make the meaning much more clear than with the traditional context. The questions of the identity of a John who is described as a prophet would be answered as John the Baptist since no other person described as a prophet is known from the first century. Likewise, the concept of someone "coming soon" who is going to bring a great message would be Jesus Christ in about 27, since that is the only messenger and message that has such importance in the first century. The concept that someone else came is not meaningful unless there was another message that was recorded at least in the 1900 years since that time, but it hasn't happened. There is a repetition of the phrase "every race, language, people and nation" as a group involved in salvation or as people who should hear the message, which would only mean the Gentiles. There is no need to use that expression at the end of the first century when Christianity had been opened to Gentiles. However, it would have been very important to explain it to Judaism before the coming of the Messiah since they believed they should remain separate from Gentiles.

This commentary has its origin in the works of Ford and Corsini even though the argumentation will rely almost entirely on examination of the Old Testament quotations and their contexts and on the context of the New Testament period of the first century. There are not a great many direct quotations from either author in this commentary and often this commentary is in conflict with the conclusions of both books. However, the concepts that go beyond Ford and Corsini, even when they present quite a different view, spring from their exceedingly adept insights.

The actual early context used in this commentary should be identified as follows:

1. Revelation describes the whole plan of God for creation and reveals the changes which would come with the Messiah and the conclusion of the plan.
2. The vision of John would be prior to the public life of the Messiah or in perhaps 25-26.
3. The writing was originally in Aramaic and done in the time of John the Baptist or by his disciples shortly after his death.
4. The Aramaic original was translated into Greek by one of his disciples whose first language was Aramaic and, therefore, was translated quite literally. The translation would have occurred in the 50s or 60s and gives traces of additions to explain certain aspects of the meaning to that new audience without changing the original text.
5. The community of John the Evangelist would have been given a copy of the Greek translation in Asia Minor probably during the time of the Jewish revolt in 66-73. The importance of the writing at that time is that it would have answered questions that arose in Christian circles concerning the destruction of the temple in 70.

This list is not determined from some known events or direct evidence from history. The items arise from the examination of the Book and, at least one factor, the translation into Greek, from the need to explain the exceedingly poor Greek texts and the presence of some explanatory details not obtained from the vision.

The first point—the whole plan of God—seems apparent from the seven seals on a scroll coming from the right hand of God on the throne (5:1). Once that conclusion is made, the view of the writing changes dramatically since the starting point for determining the meaning cannot come at the end of the first century. For Christians, the knowledge of the whole plan of God must emanate from the coming of Christ. That may not have been so clear prior to the writing of the Gospel of John, but no other conclusion seems possible after the Gospel's emphasis on Jesus' divinity. The divinity identification of Jesus is read back into the earlier writings of the New Testament without actually changing the text, but it is a change in Christian understanding of Jesus that could not be ignored in later writings. In a similar manner, the traditional context that has a focus on persecution makes no sense after the Gospel of John, and very little sense even before. There already had been the persecution of Nero that severely affected Christianity and that had been addressed in Mark's Gospel. Why would the threat of another persecution demand some new revelation from heaven? That type of assumption seems to ignore the whole meaning of the coming of Christ and his sacrifice on the cross for the salvation of humanity.

The second point about the time of the vision is derived directly from Josephine Ford's work in the Anchor Bible book Revelation.[10]

The third point proposing an Aramaic original of the writing is necessary to explain the Aramaic thought process that is seen in the text and the need to use Old Testament quotations and allusions to explain the meaning of the writing. Such a text would be written to a Jewish community since that was the only type of community John the Baptist would have had contact with during his ministry. His disciples would have knowledge of John's designation of Jesus as the Messiah. Two of John the Baptist's disciples became disciples of Jesus, Andrew mentioned by name, and the other would most likely have been John the son of Zebedee. The suggestion of a very early writing makes it unnecessary to treat chapters 12 to 22 as a later writing by disciples of John the Baptist as proposed by Josephine Ford. All of the mentions of Jesus in those chapters would fit very well with the relationship of John the Baptist with Jesus that can be seen easily in the Fourth Gospel and also, to some extent, in the Synoptic Gospels.

The fourth point of the early context is the translation of the writing into Greek by someone who would think in Aramaic and not be skilled in Greek. Such a translation would tend to be literal and provide evidence of the original language. That literalness would come as well from the fact that what is being described in the text is a vision of God and heaven. Such a document would not be treated as a subject in which a change of language would be made with a great freedom of expression. That might limit who would even be allowed to make the translation. The community of John the Baptist would go beyond a small group of disciples performing baptisms with John the Baptist. Pilgrims who came to Jerusalem for the major feasts prior to Jesus' public life might well have accepted baptism from John the Baptist and his disciples. The change of heart they were asked to accept carried no commitment other than keeping the Law very completely and accepting the Messiah when he became known. Any Jew making a pilgrimage to Jerusalem would agree to such an understanding of repentance. That Paul met some disciples who had accepted John's baptism, as did Apollos who was preaching about the Messiah, shows that Greek-speaking Jews had been opened to John's ministry (Acts 18:24-19:7). Additions that could have been made for clarification to a different audience would include statements that don't seem to come from the vision and, therefore, give clues to the date of the translation. The most apparent additions made for clarification rather than being from the vision itself would be 13:18, 16:15 and 17:9-11.

The last point about the community of John the Evangelist is a speculation that is addressed further in the Epilogue to the commentary. However, it would seem clear that if a question arose about the meaning of the destruction of the temple, a writing that explained the introduction of the Messiah from a time prior to His coming and showed that the destruction was in the plan of God would provide a dramatic answer. If the Book were available to the Greek-speaking church at the time of the Jewish revolt, it would become a very important writing. That would be a time of great interest about the cause of the temple destruction which could be answered from the Book. It would explain why Revelation was the most quoted book in the second century and later would provide support that it be included in the New Testament. This last point is not necessary for understanding the Book of Revelation but it provides the basis for a tradition of its public introduction near the end of the first century and from the community of John the Evangelist.

DATES OF THE VISION AND THE WRITING

A writing in Scripture normally is dated by the end point of the writing. Often some earlier dates might be proposed for parts of a writing, but the final composition or even redaction sets the meaning of the final composition. That pattern is most clearly seen in the Gospels where the actual teachings come from the time of Jesus Christ's public life. These stories were written down and circulated after the Resurrection as indicated by the acceptance of a "Q" document. However, the meaning of each Gospel composition as a whole is determined by the context of when those individual writings were used to address a church problem, such as Mark's Gospel responding to questions raised by Nero's persecution among those who survived the ordeal.

In Revelation the situation seems to be uniquely different if the writing is accepted as it is given, which is surely as a record of the meaning of a vision. The author indicates that he is invited to witness a vision with several scenes or a series of visions. The written presentation gives the impression that nearly all of the parts of the vision came in a single continuous sequence. However, the term "vision" is not used in the Book but only the statements that "I saw" or "what was revealed." Inspiration could be described as a series of visions and could be a result of a slower and, therefore, longer process of coming to know about a revelation. Yet that is not indicated in the text nor is it consistent with the seemingly urgent need to understand and proclaim what is being revealed.

Those urgent warnings indicate that the true context of the message would be from the time of the vision or the inspiration described as a vision. While there are statements about "writing" even as the vision is being seen, the term "writing" could more easily be seen as having the meaning of "proclaiming" and its urgency. The recording could come at a later time. However, the exceedingly poor Greek argues for an early Aramaic recording which is later translated into Greek. Without that initial definition in a relatively crude language, such as Aramaic, the Greek would be much more correct than is the present document.

A later recording of the vision in Greek or, most likely, its translation into Greek, would be a time for including some hints to how it is to be understood. Those inclusions would tend to provide clues to a later date for the Greek composition. Yet, if the vision has its meaning determined by its own context, attempting to date the vision by clues from a later translation would obscure the meaning of the entire writing. The wide variation and almost cryptic comments that occur in commentaries that use a context from a later date seem to bear out the fallacy of not examining the meaning of the vision in its own context.

Naturally, many commentaries are based on the view that there was no earlier vision or inspiration which is being described in the Book. The vision is considered to be some type of literary device to suggest an earlier time for the inspiration or the setting, while in reality, the writing occurred after the fact of some persecution or reign of a later first century emperor. The assumption is made that the writer knows what happened but, after the fact, tells a story as if what occurred had become known through an earlier foretelling of the future. Once a commentator has made that assumption, there is little need to examine the vision as an actual event. Perhaps such an approach could be justified if the proclamation of an urgent message was followed by a fulfillment of the warning. However, after nearly two thousand years, when everyone who uses that basis for examining the text is still waiting for something to occur, the suspicion must arise that what was proposed in such a commentary isn't going to happen.

The alternative would be to look at an earlier time in the first century as a context for the vision and determine if something occurred that could be seen as a revelation from God that was particularly important to all of humanity as the vision suggests. Certainly Christians would think that the coming of Jesus as the Messiah would be such an event. For that to be the actual subject would require that the vision be meaningful to Judaism since it was to them that the Messiah came and taught about the fulfillment of the Old Testament revelation. There is no need to question if there was any indication that the Jewish people received a prophecy as a warning since the four gospels state the case so clearly in the sections involving John the Baptist. It would seem that every Christian would recognize the need to examine Revelation in the context of an early writing once that possibility is raised. The context should be when a prophet came to announce that someone would come with a much greater message from heaven as is stated at the opening of the Book (1:1-2) and emphasized again at its closing (22:6-7,10).

There would be a need for some type of revelatory understanding to be given to John the Baptist prior to Jesus' public life. In Luke's Gospel, the benedictus of Zechariah (Lk 1:67-79) is a statement given in response to the Holy Spirit that John the Baptist would become a prophet with a message that introduces the coming of the Messiah. However that statement is composed, it is surely the intent of the Evangelist to say that some revelation was given to John the Baptist at the start of his public life (Lk 3:2). John knows some of the details of the coming of the Messiah and makes them part of his message (Lk 3:15-18) even if he cannot describe specifically the identity of the Messiah (Jn 1:31). Later John will question if Jesus is in fact the "one who is to come" (Lk 7:18-30) and the answer is given in a quotation from Isaiah (32:3-4). This would indicate that John may have questioned Jesus' identity based on how well he fulfilled Old Testament expectations, but also from the view of the King of Kings given to John in the vision (19:11-16). The inclusion of a record of the vision in the New Testament writings is something that should be expected and would be far more important than a late writing concerning a persecution when that subject had already been addressed in Mark's Gospel.

VISION IN AN OLD TESTAMENT DESCRIPTION

A view that can be taken of the response of John to the vision is that he is writing down everything that he saw as if taking notes during a movie (1:11 and 10:4). At the end of the vision, the final writing, or at least some very complete notes, might have been prepared and was ready for distribution (22:6-7). However, the meaning of the term "write down" also could be to proclaim the message and to do so in a very complete way. The message should go far beyond just where John could carry it and tell it by himself. Therefore, it is not necessary to take the writing as being completed on the spot or that the vision is described from the start in Old Testament allusions and quotations.

The message would be understood and remembered in some way by John whether it were a movie-like presentation in a period of hours or even a series of inspirations that would become known over a considerably longer period of time and, perhaps, only would become clear after much reflection. Such a "becoming clear" after reflection is the normal understanding of inspiration. The telling of what the vision or inspiration meant would be of little interest to Judaism if it wasn't directly related to their covenant with God. The proclamation given by John would not be given by repeating a simple oral description of a movie. Rather, it would have to be expressed in what it meant for Judaism at the very time in which they were looking forward to a Messiah and in which history records the coming of Jesus Christ who fulfilled the role of a Jewish Messiah and very much more.

The meaning of the message and the vision could only be related in terms of the covenant record from the Old Testament. It would not be just a relating of a message from Jewish history, but the only way that the unique religious meaning could be expressed. Judaism would have great interest in a message that grew out of their Scripture and their expectations. They would tend to shun any message that seemed as a replacement for their covenant relationship, even though each previous addition of revelation did exactly that. John had been opened to the plan of God and would proclaim that plan to the people who know the only True God and had been prepared for its meaning. The whole plan of God would have to include the revelation that preceded the coming of a messiah. There are no words that could express such a meaning except ones from the Old Testament.

For those who see Revelation as a writing at the very end of the New Testament writings, a whole different understanding would need to be used. Christians had come to a very different view of the Jewish covenant and the human relationship with God. The New Testament writing is a means of expressing that great difference in understanding by the end of the first century, yet that language is almost missing from Revelation. The few connective traces that can be found are either where the New Testament uses Old Testament ideas or where Christian writing seems to know something about views expressed in Revelation. Since John was ordered to "not keep the prophecies of this book secret" (22:10), for us to find some cross-connections between Revelation and the other New Testament writing is both understandable and expected if Revelation is the first part of the New Testament message. To find only a few such connections when Revelation is the last of the New Testament writings has no meaning whatsoever.

The start of the mission of John the Baptist would be in a proclamation of the coming of the Messiah and the need for the Jewish people to live out the covenant relationship more fully. The message was to change (repent) because "the kingdom of heaven is close at hand" (Mt 3:2). For such a situation there would be a need under the Law to do something as a means of acceptance. The passing through the water of the Jordan River even though on dry land marked the original entry into the promised land (Jos 3:17); John's baptism would be an individual passing through the Jordan to enter the new kingdom given by

God. However, the people would be responding to their own historical understanding of that kingdom. John's understanding from the vision is that some retribution would occur because of how the Old Testament covenant was being kept and that the people would be called beyond that covenant. He sees the "kingdom of God" coming as a judgment day situation with harsh punishments for those who had failed in the existing covenant and says as much to Jewish leaders (Mt 3:7-12). How much fuller the message must have been is not known outside of Revelation because the Gospel accounts that provide greater information about the kingdom reflect the period of Jesus' public life or after when the message became known more fully.

A searching of the Old Testament for quotations to state the full meaning of the vision or inspiration would take some time but would likely occur as John the Baptist gained disciples who needed to be taught more fully. They would be the recipients of the more complete message and would produce the requirement that it be put into writing. A message given in this type of format would have to be put in writing since it is a collection of understandings to be studied, rather than a true narrative that can be repeated easily and clearly. John would give the explanation in terms of what the message meant to Judaism and those explanations would be recorded in terms of what God had revealed earlier. In John's Gospel, Jesus, Peter, Andrew and probably John, the son of Zebedee, with Philip and Nathaniel appear to be closely associated with John the Baptist and at least two of them were his disciples. The full message might be passed on to them even though they may not have been a party to the written document.

The original writing would have been in Aramaic and kept in that language for a long time after John the Baptist's death. However, by 53 Paul met disciples of John in Ephesus who had not been baptized into the Christian Church even though they seem to consider themselves followers of the Messiah (Acts 19:1-7). Apollos also considered himself a disciple of the Messiah (Acts 18:24-28) even though experiencing only the baptism of John. The disciples of John clearly had moved beyond Palestine. It would be assumed that such disciples might originate from Greek-speaking Jews who were baptized by John while visiting Jerusalem for annual feasts rather than being Palestinian Jews who had carried John's message to Greek-speaking lands.

At some point, the Aramaic record of John's vision or inspiration would require translation into Greek. The rather literal translation into Greek would come from John's Palestinian disciples to produce the poor Greek text that has become part of the New Testament. However, once that translation was made and received some minor distribution, it would present a view that was different from a Christian view which for some time after the Resurrection seemed to include remnants of an early second coming to set up a kingdom. Mark's Gospel shows that the second coming is clearly a last judgment event (13:24-27), meaning that the seeming lack of a second coming was still being questioned or at last answered in Jesus' own words. Then the destruction of the temple in 70 would have raised the question to Jews and all Jewish Christians, or perhaps all Christians, if that event meant God was displeased with the chosen people. That seemed to be the thought within Judaism when the temple was destroyed at the time of the exile to Babylon. Revelation would demonstrate that this second destruction was in the plan of God and that the message from heaven was to "come away from her" (18:4) rather than be concerned. The translation of the vision meaning into Greek could have occurred at that time, but it is more likely that the translation was earlier and only some notations to clarify some meanings (13:18) would have been added in the translation.

READING THE COMMENTARY

OUTLINE OF THE BOOK OF REVELATION

The structure of the Book of Revelation can be seen quite easily as determined by a series of sevens. The number seven is stated often in the Book and there are additional uses of groups containing seven elements even if the number is not stated. The number seven means completeness in apocalyptic writing and its dominant use would tend to indicate that the Book is something complete or the completion of something. Such a meaning becomes very important if the Book is a revelation of the whole plan of God for creation as seen in chapters four, five and six which introduce the start of creation and in the last two chapters when creation has disappeared.

Every commentary on Revelation reflects an understanding of the importance of the sevens and many examine that meaning, but seem to leave the subject without a distinctive conclusion. Often the sevens are noted in an introduction without following through in reflecting that importance in the actual commentary section. Even the Anchor Bible book <u>Revelation</u>, which is one of the most comprehensive examination of all the writings on Revelation, doesn't seem to make a definite conclusion. One approach suggested in that study is seven series of sevens, surely the type of completeness that one would seek, yet only two of the seven actually contain a full seven.[11] A second approach which is suggested as "attractive" has six series of six which tends to mean incompletion.[12] What is at first considered to be a part of the writing with an obvious importance is not used that way with any certainty in commentaries.

Other commentators take the obvious groups of seven—letters, seals, trumpets, and bowls—as a starting point and often fill in with one or two groups of seven that are unnumbered. The first unnumbered group is made up of events and identifications found between the trumpets and the bowls. A second group of seven such scenes is found between the bowls and the heavenly Jerusalem. Such a system of six sets of seven is the most logical use of the text but ending with only six sets, a condition explicitly incomplete, presents a problem. However, proposals to produce seven sets of seven are unconvincing.

The structure of this commentary, to the extent such a definition is necessary, would follow the use of six sets of seven that differ only slightly from what is used in other commentaries.

They would be identified as follows:

Introduction to the Book	Chapter 1
Seven Letters	Chapters 2 and 3
Introduction to the Visions in Heaven	Chapters 4 and 5
Seven Seals	Chapters 6 to 8:1
Seven Trumpets	Chapters 8:2 - 11:1
Seven Unnumbered Visions	Chapters 12 - 14
(woman, dragon, sea beast, earth beast, Lamb's companions, angels, judgment)	
Seven Bowls	Chapters 15 and 16
Seven Unnumbered Visions	Chapters 17 - 20
(harlot, people summoned, first battle, dragon subjugated, one thousand years, second battle, final judgment)	
Completeness of Creation in Heaven	Chapters 21 - 22:5
Sending of the Prophet	Chapter 22:6-21

This system has only six sevens during the time in which creation exists, with the final completeness (or a seven in apocalyptic terminology) occurring in heaven. The two unnumbered series could be identified differently in how the subject matter is divided. However, the seventh trumpet and seventh bowl are clearly oriented to the coming of judgment and the same could be inferred for the undescribed seventh seal. Therefore, the end point of each unnumbered seven is placed at a judgment scene to maintain a similar ending.

There are three sections in Revelation which are introduced unambiguously as sevens: the seven seals (5:1), seven trumpets (8:2), and seven bowls (15:7). Each of these are described as a seven and the descriptions of their use are listed in a one-through-seven sequence. So the author's meaning of them is indisputable. The seven letters are somewhat different in that there is no statement that there are seven letters. There is a reference to a book or a scroll that is to be written and sent to seven churches (1:11), meaning the complete church, but no mention of seven letters. There are seven writings in chapters two and three but no designation that the writings are a list of one through seven. The most that could be said about the letters is that they have an undefined completeness in themselves but have a designated completeness only in being written to the whole church. Even that level of completeness is left unclear since the letters do not constitute a book and so the command to write a "book and send it to seven churches" would most likely mean the Book of Revelation or at least the section from chapters four through 22:12.

There are two series of seven which are neither called a seven nor have a listing of one through seven nor are shown as clearly distinctive elements of such a list. The first of these two series is placed between the seven trumpets and the seven bowls starting with the woman in heaven as a sign (12:1-6) and ending in a judgment sequence (14:14-20). Since all of the series of seven mentioned earlier end in a judgment or divine coming into creation scene, it might be reasonable to accept this first unnumbered sequence as an actual seven. However, there doesn't seem to be any real agreement among scholars that such a conclusion is supported. Without any significant mention or designation as a seven, the conclusion would be that the term "completeness" should not be attached to this unnumbered series even though they could be part of a system of sevens, and, therefore, be the fourth of the system of sevens. A second unnumbered and undesignated series comes after the seven bowls, starting with the harlot and ending with judgment and punishment. The ending in a judgment as seen on earth would be the final part of each of the six series of sevens. Naturally, the "six series" on earth would not be completeness of the plan of God by themselves so the "six" could be appropriate.

The heavenly Jerusalem would then be cast as the seventh seven, the eternal completeness which does indeed complete God's plan for creation. It occurs after creation disappears so the plan of God for creation has concluded. The eternal reward does not reflect a list of one through seven, but certainly the meaning of completeness is overwhelmingly obvious. The final day for creation is an eternal time with God rather than efforts related to creation. So then the final stage of creation as seen by humanity would be the eternal time with God rather than steps related to reaching the climax of life for creation.

The letters are treated in this commentary as something that could have been added to the description of the vision, perhaps at the time of the translation to make clear that the vision could not be understood without the Old Testament background. However, if the letters are a later addition, the original number of sevens would be reduced to five and make the completeness of heaven a sixth completeness. That would be an unacceptable conclusion if the author was carefully constructing the completeness theme into the Book. This raises the question of how complicated and precise the structure was intended to be by the author and how much is the creation of commentators. As will be seen in the commentary that follows, the choosing of an early context tends to make many parts of this Book simple, direct and clear rather than what occurs from using the traditional context. Perhaps the Book was meant to reveal the plan of God for creation very clearly as we should expect from the instructions at its start and again at its conclusion. Surely the profusion of Old Testament quotations and allusions would be intended to instruct Jews in terms that were clearly part of their heritage.

This structure would support the proposal that Revelation is about the whole plan of God which also is seen in the text. In doing so, it provides a framework that assists in the interpretation of each part of the writing in the commentary. Certainly a concept of the whole plan of God makes a second coming to set up a kingdom meaningless as does also the Gospel of John. Likewise, the view that this writing is about late first century persecutions falls by the wayside. This becomes the book which introduces the Messiah to Judaism in the context of their whole history. The revelation mentioned in the first verse and used as a title is the revelation brought by Jesus Christ. As the early church expectations of a second coming disappeared, acceptance of Christians by Judaism ended as well and separation would result between Judaism and Christianity. This Book could be read by the early church after the opening to Gentiles had been accomplished and the temple was destroyed, and its message would be that all of those changes and their results were intended by God and made known even before the coming of the Messiah. The changes were all part of the plan of God from the start and the Church should continue with its mission.

NUMBERS AND SYMBOLS

Apocalyptic writing often includes the use of numbers and symbols to express meanings in a way which is separate from the words themselves. This has the look of being a code that might keep the message from outsiders who do not understand the code and, therefore, restrict the meaning only to insiders to whom the writing is actually addressed. However, the numbers and symbols used in Revelation are a type that commonly would be known in the first century. They may not limit the meaning from outsiders to any great extent but could have a special emphasis which would be missed by a modern reader.

The number seven is the most important number in the writing and always carries a meaning of completeness. The modern tendency would be an attempt to define the meaning of each of a list of seven rather than to recognize that "seven" often should just be replaced by the word "complete" to some extent. In chapter five a scroll which has seven seals is given to the Lamb and as each seal is opened an event occurs with some meaning. However, the initial meaning of the scroll seems to be that it is the plan of God for all of creation. Therefore, the designation "seven seals" has some meaning, such as, it is completely sealed, or since a seal validates a document, it is a completely valid plan, or, most likely, it is a complete plan. The meaning of completeness at the start of the designation is important in understanding the meaning of the seven events that follow rather than the other way around. The seven events or items in the vision that result from opening the seven seals do not provide the complete meaning even when proclaimed in the seven trumpets or implemented in the seven bowls. The meaning of completeness comes from the designation of "seven" rather than the totality of the individual explanations that follow.

There are other series of events in the writing which can be listed as a series of seven but are not designated by the number seven. The clearest example of an undesignated seven is the seven letters which are never called "seven letters." John is told to write a book to the seven churches and seven cities are then named (1:11); however, that does not call for seven letters to be written even though they are addressed to the same cities. Such a series of seven letters would not carry the meaning of completeness as a designated seven and should be seen as some other type of explanation rather than something which is "complete." The interpretation of a designated seven always carries a special meaning while a simple list of seven items would not mean complete.

The numbers four and three which make up the sevens relate to earth and heaven almost as if to say that completeness is everything on earth and in heaven. The number four is often used for earth even in present everyday language in such terms as the four directions, four winds, four corners of the earth and, perhaps, a great many others. The first four of the seven in seals, trumpets, and bowls are all related to earth and probably represent what is natural or expected on earth. A difference exists in the first seal in that the white horse event appears to be what God intended in the first of four rather than what might seem natural after the original fall from grace.

The number three relates to heaven but not in the same way as the Trinity reflects heaven. The Trinity is far beyond creation and so the heaven represented by three includes created beings from outside of what humans would see as creation. Therefore, three includes angels which are created and understood as sometimes coming to earth, and it includes evil spirits which must have been created as angels but chose not to live as they were intended. These evil spirits are removed from the presence of God and show up on earth (12:7-9), but they are still part of the three. Likewise, the water of the abyss is part of creation but appears as a leftover from the original act of creation when the primeval water was pushed aside and dry land appeared and was populated. So the beast coming from the sea results from something with connection to the three (13:1), while the false prophet from the ground would be a response to the beast that comes from creation (13:11).

The fifth of the sevens relates to evil coming to earth and the sixth of each seven shows the effects of humanity accepting the guidance of such evil and what results on earth. The seventh of each seven involves the divine action of judging or, more clearly, God coming into the created area of humanity as creation is destroyed. Therefore, the three that relate to heaven actually include the situation where spiritual life, not part of the creation made for human use, comes into the human domain. The coming of God is the whole meaning of the plan in that humanity has a direct relationship with God in a sharing of God's presence and that is a movement beyond creation for humanity.

The number six by itself is not part of the vision, but is used by a later writer to provide a clue to the meaning of the beast (13:18). Since six is one less than completion, it has a meaning of incompleteness and, especially, an incompleteness which is deliberately determined. If the final part of a seven is God's presence coming into creation, the six has an understanding of deliberately excluding or ignoring God in the plan for creation. It is an incompleteness which eliminates God and, therefore, is evil. In the identity clue to the beast, a triple six is used to develop the superlative of most evil, and the meaning may not go beyond such a conclusion.

A number ten refers to fullness rather than completeness. The ten commandments would be considered as the fullness of commandments, but the commandments are not the totality or completeness of the relationship with God which in Judaism also includes the Law, the temple and Scripture. Fullness in Revelation occurs with the kings who exercise worldly power at a particular time but are not the complete presence of earthly kings for the whole plan of God. Fullness is less than completeness but that is not the true comparison. Fullness can occur in certain situations but only what refers to the whole of the Revelation can be called completeness.

The number twelve always refers to the fullness of Israel, the twelve tribes, or later as Judaism. In the heavenly court (4:4) there is a circle of twenty-four elders present. That group would be a double fullness of Israel or Judaism and is noted but not explained in the vision. That double fullness of Israel could best be explained as the priests and prophets of Israel. Israel and Judaism could be identified with the keeping of the Law as the covenant relationship which involves the priests at the temple. The identification also could be seen in the prophets which in the Jewish understanding would include the kings and leaders, as former prophets, and the written prophets as the later prophets. They would represent Judaism as the people of Israel living the covenant relationship. There would always be both a keeping of the temple prescriptions in the Law and also the leading and guidance of the nation. The lack of leaders that seems to occur after the Exile is only a result of Judaism developing into a religion that didn't require leaders of the kingdom in Palestine, but was developing toward the kingdom intended for the whole world.

The use of thousand is the statement of a great but undetermined magnitude. It is not meant to be an approximation of a number that cannot be determined, but a truly undetermined number that could be more than one could know or perhaps one of such a magnitude so as to have a "why bother to count" meaning.

A second type of number is one identified as three and one-half years, 42 months or 1,260 days, with some variations. If the complete time of the plan of God for creation would be a seven in some form, this number would be half of that total period. If seven years, the completeness of years or of time, represents the total time, the half time would be half of that and could be expressed in years, months, or days. This would represent a time of testing but in some commentaries it is often considered as a time of persecution. However, the persecution never would have lasted for half of the total time of the plan of God. Even its use as persecution for the more than three years of the Maccabees revolt, from the time when a pagan statue was placed in the Jerusalem temple until its rededication in 164 BC, would not be an apocalyptic meaning. That concept would come from those commentators who treat Daniel as a prophecy after the fact so that the entire period of the event was known before the writing and the correct number inserted into the account. Most likely Daniel would be written in symbolic language that gives the true meaning from a religious standpoint rather than an approximation of an exact time. Judaism would see a period of both trial and reward, where the two would be in balance, more easily than the use of symbolic numbers for something known exactly. Therefore, the half time should be considered symbolic in Daniel and that meaning is carried over to Revelation in the quotations. The importance of this writing and the coming of a Messiah should be seen in terms of the whole plan of God rather than a short period of earlier persecution.

OLD TESTAMENT QUOTATIONS

A major objection to assigning a late date to the writing of Revelation, at the very end of the New Testament period, is the overwhelming use of Old Testament quotations and allusions. It has been estimated that the 404 verses contain from about 250 to over 500 such quotations and allusions. However, the use of such connections to the New Testament writings are very few and often only to New Testament quotes which are themselves a reflection of Old Testament quotations. Not only are there few New Testament connections but the Book makes excessive use of the Old Testament meanings to describe the vision. This discrepancy overwhelmingly points to an author with only an Old Testament knowledge and a similar audience.

If the writing is an introduction to the initial coming of the Messiah, the Old Testament is the essential reference for Judaism. They would not accept anyone who just showed up with a message that promoted a change in the covenant relationship. There would have to be a strong connection to their historical relationship with God for the teaching to be accepted and presenting it in concepts from the Old Testament would be a logical approach. Even Jesus who came with a message of great change had to start his teaching from an Old Testament base.

The vision itself would be in images rather than words except for statements or explanations by elders or others who are called angels in the vision. The written description of the text would come from the writer who could be John the Baptist or one of his disciples. John the Baptist would give a broader message about the coming than is recorded in the Gospel sections that relate to him. Surely he would have explained the whole concept of the vision more completely to his disciples. There are some indications that John's disciples saw him as the Messiah and may have promoted that concept even for some time after John's death. His message would have been something to be saved and used just like the words of any earlier prophet.

As questions arose from his disciples and from the people, they would be answered from scriptural quotations or allusions. The mining of the Old Testament for the descriptions is no different from what was done by Jesus' disciples in identifying fulfillment prophecies to show that Jesus was the Messiah who was expected. The meaning of what was seen in the vision would come from how it could be shown as conforming to what was known from Scripture. The people coming for baptism would be more likely to respond to what was referenced directly from the word of God than however well the story was told by the prophet. The very strength of the response to John the Baptist as shown in the New Testament indicates wide acceptance that the message was sent from God.

An early record of the vision would have been Aramaic, the common language used even in the synagogues of Palestine for preaching and explanations. Once John the Baptist had been martyred, the record of the vision and its meaning would not be changed to any great extent. That would create a difficulty in producing a later translation into correct Greek. The translation process could have been quite literal, by a disciple whose first language was Aramaic, and resulted in a text that is clearly the worst Greek in the New Testament.

The Old Testament quotations are a more major source of meaning than the numbers suggest. Often they carry the conclusion of a much longer section of the Old Testament and so have far greater meaning than the few words of the quotation would indicate. It is reasonable to argue that the audience of the Book would only grasp its meaning from the Old Testament connections. Only in showing that the vision in Revelation has its meaning from the previous revelation to Judaism would the Book be acceptable. So the clarity of the message comes from its Old Testament descriptions and its validity requires the showing that it follows on from the Old Testament rather than being an independent revelation.

READING THE COMMENTARY

The detailed commentary that follows requires a certain amount of study and a great amount of cross-checking with the biblical text of Revelation and the rest of Scripture. It would be helpful to read through the entire Book of Revelation, in a single sitting if possible, prior to starting on the commentary. An important element in understanding any book of Scripture is an attempt to see the whole writing at the same time. A reading of the Book prior to starting a detailed analysis or just before following the text through a commentary provides that whole view even as one examines the parts.

Revelation does not follow a time sequence like most other writings. The sequence of the major sevens—seals, trumpets and bowls—are each in a time sequence from creation to judgment with the first four starting at the time of creation of humanity and then continuing in time. The fifth and sixth are later than the start of creation and the seventh brings judgment so it is at the end of creation. The three major sevens are a repetition of each other rather than trumpets following seals or bowls being a final sequence. They are three different views, each with a different purpose and different details. The first set of unnumbered visions follow the same overall time sequence and give additional background from the Old Testament record for that time sequence. The second set of unnumbered visions provides the same type of detail for future events starting at the time of the visions and ending in judgment. Therefore, there are repetitions of some of the same events from one set of visions to another. References are included in the commentary to tie back to previous descriptions of the same events and also forward to later descriptions of the same events. Having read through the text before starting the commentary will prepare the reader for such forward references by becoming familiar with the entire text prior to starting.

Time has great meaning within creation but is far less important in heaven. The plan of God has been completed prior to anything actually shown in the vision. So the sequence of events will not be oriented to time directly. Only when the events occur in creation are they recorded as historical events in time. Some of the writing is about God's intentions and given in general terms while the intrusion of those intentions into creation will result in a record of historical events.

The fact is that nothing actually happens in Revelation but everything is about examining and recording a vision that describes the whole plan of God. This interferes with the determination of how events fit into sequential and historical relationships with each other. Clearly, the seven seals, trumpets and bowls are different views of the same sequences. They show how the sequence unfolded in the plan of God, how they are announced in heaven and how they impact on earth. However, each of these is shown through the eyes and understanding of John even if explained by an angel in the vision. The double series of seven unnumbered visions is similar with the first being a past series known in part through the history of Israel and the Old Testament revelation. The second series describes what is to come at the time of the vision but some of it would be recognized as having come by the time the writing and translation is complete.

There is, however, a description of events which doesn't place everything in a consistent historical procession. The destruction of the harlot is completed in the section where she is described, yet her destruction historically occurs after the death and resurrection of Jesus Christ even though that event is mentioned both in chapter 17 and then again as part of the victory over the beast (Chap 19) which follows the destruction of Jerusalem in the text. Revelation is the vision telling how the whole plan of God will show up in history rather than a description in a single historical sequence. The same could be said about the meaning of the seven letters which gives the Israelite-Jewish history and must be seen as a starting point for all understanding of the plan of God. If this description of the Revelation is being presented to Christians in Asia Minor then they have to see it as their starting point not as a Jewish Old Testament teaching. The places where the history occurred is not as important as how the Old Testament people were led to the place in history where they were ready for the last part of the revelation to come in the life of the Messiah.

The community of John the Evangelist by the time of the writing may have existed in Ephesus for some period of time and, perhaps, a great many of the community were converts from that area. The background is placed in their area to show they have to see themselves as descendants of the people of the Old Testament. They must be just as responsible for their decisions of accepting the revelation of Jesus Christ based on the same background as the Jewish people had in the actual occurrence of those events and Jesus' public life. The plan of God is not just about Jewish history or about accepting a greatly revised messiah understanding from what had been recorded in the Old Testament. The entire Revelation must be considered as the message from God, including that which was already recorded at the time of the Messiah and gained its completeness from the Messiah.

Therefore, in the commentary some details will be given a very short explanation and the record of some events in the history of the Israelites and at the time of Jesus will be noted in a citation from the Old Testament. However, some explanations will be quite long when it involves a more complex historical development. These longer explanations will interrupt the commentary to some extent but will probably be clearer than to have a greater explanation of such development before the commentary starts and expect the reader to fit the early explanations into the commentary text simply by remembering. Again, an initial reading of the text of Revelation prior to starting on the commentary will eliminate many of these difficulties.

BOOK OF REVELATION

CHAPTER 1 - Introduction

A brief examination of the Book of Revelation quickly shows a great variation in how Jesus Christ is mentioned at the start of the Book and again at the very end and how he is hardly mentioned, and done so less directly, in between. Jesus Christ, as a designation which is common from the time of Paul's writings, occurs only three times in the Book and those are in verses one, two and five of chapter one.[13] Moreover, the text doesn't support a late understanding of Jesus Christ, certainly not the understanding of a Divine Jesus as shown in John's Gospel.

The opening verse describes the revelation as being given by God to Jesus Christ who could then pass it on to his servants rather than to disciples, the term used in the Gospels. The verse includes the type of language which has separation between God and Jesus Christ that would fit an early understanding of a human messiah or prophet rather than a Divine Messiah. Such separation would be acceptable in an early context, but would not fit any context after the time of John's Gospel when the church would know of Jesus' divinity. It is clear, both in the New Testament as a whole and in this Book (10:4), that the great message, "seven claps of thunder" or something from heaven, is the message that is brought by Jesus to his "servants." That message to John would be the vision given in this Book in which the one speaking is described as an angel (7:2, 10:1, 22:6-13) or as a voice from heaven. So the introduction identifies Jesus as the Messiah who brings the revelation to others in the gospel proclaimed in his public life, but John has been visited by a special messenger or "angel" who makes known to him the message in this vision which John writes down. It fits the view we have of John the Baptist in the Gospels of proclaiming the coming of the Messiah before Jesus' public life when the great revelation becomes known. Commentaries that use the traditional context, at the end of the first century, often indicate that the revelation which is the subject of this first introduction is the record of the vision. The text of this introduction or of the Book doesn't support such a conclusion. The revelation given by Jesus Christ is the Gospel.

A second introduction in verse five shows even greater separation between God and Jesus Christ where grace and peace come first from God ("Who is, who was and who is to come" which would be the Divine name in the Old Testament and used by Jesus for himself in John's Gospel 8:58); second, from seven spirits (rather than the Holy Spirit but having the same meaning) and, third, from Jesus Christ. In the New Testament only the First Letter of Peter arranges the trinitarian formula with the Holy Spirit second.

The third introduction in verse nine could be the earliest of the three since the author introduces himself as John and, while indicating a union with Jesus, has to explain that he is a brother to Christian readers. That clarification would be unnecessary if John were the author of the Fourth Gospel and this Book were written after that Gospel was known throughout Christianity. After that the active involvement of Jesus Christ by name ends except for the last six verses of the Book. There Jesus speaks in the first person (22:16) and the term "Lord Jesus" is used twice in the closing and benediction (22:20-21). The name Jesus is used six times in the body of the writing, and most could be later additions for clarity when the Book was first prepared or translated. However, John the Baptist would clearly know some of the apostles from his own personal relationship with them (Jn 1:35-42) and may have known also about them as a special group of twelve (Jn 3:22-24 and Mt 11:1-6). Therefore, some of the references to Jesus in chapters 12 through 20 would be normal references to Jesus' disciples from the time of John the Baptist or from John's own disciples who edited or translated the Book after John's death.

Some of these mentions of Jesus could be additions for clarity if the removal of the mention resulted in an understandable text. Four of the mentions of Jesus are not in the vision directly and must come from the description written by John to explain his conclusions about the vision. They are, in that case, additions to the vision just as the Old Testament quotations would be additions by John to clearly explain what the vision should mean to the Jewish people. Only the two mentions of Jesus in chapter 19 are more difficult to label as additions.

The additions could be "and bear witness for Jesus" in 12:17 after "all who obey God's commandments," "and faith in Jesus" in 14:12 after "saints who keep the commandments of God," "and the blood of the martyrs of Jesus" in 17:6 after "drunk with the blood of the saints" and "having witnessed for Jesus" in 20:4 inserted before "and for having preached God's word." Removing the name Jesus would not change the meaning of the sentences to any great extent. The additions would include holy people from the period during and after the public life of Jesus while the text without the possible additions could be seen as Old Testament people. The first of the two mentions of Jesus in 19:10 is "witnesses to Jesus" in which "to Jesus" could be a later modification but witnesses would have been the original object of the clause. The second mention of Jesus in 19:10 has "the witness Jesus gave" in which the name Jesus could not be removed without replacing it with some other subject or modifying the sentence. However, it is clear from the Gospel quotes above that Jesus gave witness during the time when John the Baptist was alive.

Therefore, the overall view of the Book is that the first nine verses and the last six verses may reflect Christian use of variations of Jesus' name, but are no different from those found in the earliest writings of the New Testament. In the remainder of the Book, the use of Jesus' name could easily come from the time of John the Baptist's ministry or be the result of adding Jesus' name for clarification when translated. However, even in the first nine and last six verses, the terminology of Jesus as the Messiah (Jesus Christ) was known by John the Baptist (Jn 3:28) and the Greek text would be a later translation when Jesus Christ would be the normal use. The remainder of the Book has the plan of God and a messianic figure described in different terminology, but without a direct indication that the figure would be Jesus the Messiah who actually was revealed to John the Baptist when he baptized Jesus (Jn 1:29-34). So in that respect, the message of the writing as a whole, with or without the initial and final verses and any "Jesus" additions, could have been known by John the Baptist during Jesus' public life.

In a more detailed examination of the text itself, the first introduction (1:1-3) tells of the giving of Revelation to John who wrote it down, with John in the third person so it seems to have been written at a later time. However, the message to John was sent by an angel, which is a Jewish view of how revelation comes from God, and tends to make even the first introduction an early writing or a statement from a Jewish source. The emphasis is on something which will happen "very soon" and the "time is close," a warning that is repeated at the end of the Book as well (22:6-7,10). What is written is called a prophecy (1:3) and is to be proclaimed. It would seem that this section would be the introduction to the entire Book, or could come from the time when the translated Book was presented to the community of John the Evangelist.

The second introduction opens with a greeting (1:4) similar to the format of New Testament letters, so it could come from the time of the translation of the Book into Greek. It is addressed to "the seven churches of Asia" so this would be the time when the seven letters would have been included, since the Revelation itself is to the whole world (10:11) and already had been given in Palestine. This introduction includes a series of titles describing Jesus Christ, but the term "Lord God" (1:8) refers to God in an Old Testament context. It does not seem that an introduction would describe Jesus in Old Testament terms or have the great separation between God and Jesus Christ if it were written after the Gospel of John. It may have been an introduction used when the record of the vision was translated. However, the primary responsibility of John the Baptist was to identify the Messiah as the fulfillment of the Old Testament and the introduction of Jesus in such terms (1:5-7) does just that.

The third introduction causes the most difficulty in interpretation since it seems to be a vision or inspiration to John to write what was made known to him in the first introduction. It would introduce chapters four to 22 since that is clearly the record of the vision. This "John" could mean John the Baptist unless the understanding of the original vision was that it was meant for the world so that a disciple of John the Baptist could address the record to any part of the world and used John's name in preparing this particular document. However, even this introduction doesn't necessarily include the seven letters. The direction is to write a book and send that to the seven churches (1:11), or to the complete church, without mentioning or intending individual letters. A later clarification of including "present happenings and things to come" (1:19) might refer to the vision which includes what is "present" for John and some future happenings. However, the letters, in any interpretation, are primarily a description of past events, which are present only in the sense of being given to John at that time but they include nothing about future events.

The letters of chapter two and three represent an intrusion into the writing since they do not reflect the instructions of the third introduction and if removed would make the text connect up quite easily with the vision of chapter four. Therefore, both the third introduction and the remainder of the Book show these letters to be an addition for understanding at the time of the translation when the Book would be introduced to the Greek-speaking world, rather than being part of the vision itself or part of an earlier record of the vision.

The third introduction identifies John as a "brother," or Christian, and a member of the kingdom (1:9). That identification would not be included if the author was John the Evangelist since he would be known as an Apostle. However, it might be appropriate for John the Baptist or a later writer in introducing John the Baptist. Certainly, he is the only John, identified as a prophet (10:11) and "much more than a prophet" (Mt 11:9-10),

that is known from the first century. The letters would not be
written by John the Baptist, so if that is the identity of John, this
introduction would occur prior to the inclusion of the letters.
As one who died early in Jesus' public life, John the Baptist
could be introduced as "brother" and member of the kingdom,
since he had the title of a Jewish prophet rather than a Christian. Reading the Gospel accounts seems to present him as a
Jewish prophet who wasn't completely sure about the identity of
Jesus as Messiah (Mt 11:2-3). Such uncertainty supports the
concept that the recording of the early vision was presented to
the community of John the Evangelist before the Fourth Gospel
was completed.

It is possible that the "John" of Revelation is someone
with that name but unknown from any other source. He could
be a disciple of John the Baptist who knows the story of the
vision and is inspired to make a record of it at some later point
in time. Paul had met disciples of John the Baptist in Ephesus as
early as 53 (Acts 19:1-7) so there is justification for such an
assumption. However, the reading of Revelation produces the
definite impression that the source for a record of the vision is
the one experiencing it with no basis for choosing a different
writer than the visionary. The early recording of the vision in
the words of the visionary would be in Aramaic, through personal writing or dictation in Aramaic, and would provide the
basic starting point for the Book. Its translation into Greek at a
later time by an Aramaic-speaking disciple who tried to follow
the Aramaic version closely would help explain the difficult
Greek text. A translator might not feel free to paraphrase a
description of a vision from heaven. It would leave room for
some additional comments in the final edition to make parts
that were clear to Palestinian Jews also understandable to
Greek-speaking Christians in Asia Minor at a later date. Such
additions would include the first introduction in chapter one
and the closing of chapter 22 and a few additions and excursions
in the body of the Book.

The command to "write down all that you see in a book"
(scroll) (1:11) has the meaning of an order to reveal the vision

or even to proclaim it. Once something is written it becomes automatically and completely revealed to anyone who reads it while something only told might be kept relatively confidential. The Book then is to be sent to the seven churches, but "seven churches" has the meaning of the complete church wherever the seven might be. What follows is a list of seven cities in the province of Asia so that could indicate that the Book is to be sent only to the "complete" church of that province but that would not be the normal use of the designation "seven." So, the translation of the Book would be directed to Asia Minor, with the names of the seven cities added in the third introduction, and perhaps it was assumed that it would go no further. However, the vision isn't limited to that area and wouldn't nec-essarily be given in that place. The island of Patmos could have the meaning of being an uninhabited or remote area, but it isn't a term that fits what John the Baptist would use for the wilder-ness in Palestine where "the word of God came" (Lk 3:2). That would mean that this introduction includes some writing which would use a coded understanding, perhaps to clarify a deeper meaning rather than to hide a meaning.

The person speaking to John (1:12-16) is described in a series of Old Testament quotations: a figure "like a son of man" (Dan 7:13), "white wool hair" (Dan 7:9), "golden girdle" (Dan 10:5), "burning eyes" (Dan 10:6), "burnished bronze feet" (Dan 10:6), and "voice like an ocean" (Ez 43:2). All are from the book of Daniel except the last and that could have been a "voice like the roar of a crowd" (Dan 10:6). However, there could be a reason for switching to Ezekiel since that quotation is about Yahweh coming to condemn the rulers of the House of Israel for defiling God's name in how sacrifices were offered. They were to be banished, but God would live among the sons of Israel forev-er. That image is one that comes from the vision in Revelation so the Ezekiel connection would be correct. Even so, there is an equating of "voices of a huge crowd" and "the sound of the ocean" later in the Book (19:6) so indirectly it ties to Daniel. The use of Old Testament quotes to describe the Messiah as the fulfillment of the earlier understandings would be necessary in an early context since the message is to Judaism. However, at the end of the New Testament period, there would be little reason to even include such quotations to identify the Messiah to other Christians.

The double-edged sharp sword coming out of his mouth is the word of God which at the time of the vision would be the Old Testament, but here could be the greater message that comes from the Messiah. Since it comes from his mouth, he would not be an angel even though that would be a normal understanding for revelation coming to Judaism. Later when John kneels to worship an angel (19:10 and 22:8), this greater message may be his understanding also in order to produce such a strange reaction. Certainly the being who is described in Daniel 10:5-6 would have seemed to be an angel and that is the source of much of the description of the speaker. After reviving the fainted John, the speaker calls himself "the First and the Last" (1:18). Yet, this is about the same title as the "Alpha and the Omega" used for God earlier (1:8). There is an equating of the speaker with God which John doesn't seem to understand from the vision, but which is made clear in the Fourth Gospel. The vision and the writing of this text are shown here also as being earlier than the Gospel, yet this part of chapter one would come from the vision and make clear the misunderstanding of John concerning the identity of the Lamb.

The seven stars are given as the seven angels of the churches which would be the completeness of angels providing messages to the churches (1:17-20). Likewise, the seven lampstands surrounding the speaker are the churches with seven referring to the completeness of the churches or the whole church. Holding the angels in his hand points toward a divine speaker and being surrounded by the seven lampstands would make the speaker the complete source of the churches themselves. The use of these Old Testament quotes, here and in verses 5-7 above, are essential for describing the Messiah by John since he hasn't seen the Messiah in this Book except as a lamb (4:6) and the rider of the white horse (19:11-16). Later, he will recognize Jesus only when the Spirit comes down on him at his baptism (Jn 1:31-34). There is no other description available to John in proclaiming the coming of the Messiah to the Jewish people, prior to the public life of Jesus. This also points to an early context for the vision and its recording.

CHAPTER 2 - Seven Letters

A difficulty that affects interpretations of the letters for any context used for the writing is that not much is actually known about the history of the seven cities. Commentaries often try to give some explanation of each verse but most are based on the commentator's assumptions and, for some, there is no other information than what is written in this Book. Worse yet is the fact that often where Old Testament quotes or allusions are used, the assumption is made that the Old Testament meaning is not retained so the explanation is based on an apocalyptic-coded meaning. In this examination of the seven letters, the Old Testament meanings are given priority since the letters seem to be a summary of the Old Testament development of Judaism. Interpretations of words or phrases that have no clear tie with Old Testament quotations will still be examined with the Old Testament development in mind. However, where no meaning is evident, it would seem that the lack of knowledge about these cities or some terms in the letters cause some meaning to be historically lost.

The letters are written not to the churches directly, but to the angels of the churches individually. That use of angel would fit the time of the Old Testament Law period when Judaism thought in terms of the Law being given through angels. However, in the conclusion of each letter a warning is given that anyone with ears should "listen to what the Spirit is saying to the churches." This language would have a Christian context in a time after the Resurrection as a means of following the way of Christ. The Holy Spirit is the source of information and it is given to all of the churches (the completeness of the churches) rather than to an individual church. Both of these views point toward the Old Testament situation that seems to be incorporated into these letters. The Spirit's warning in each letter surely is a reminder of the need to go beyond the Jewish belief in revelation as will be shown in the Book of Revelation. Jesus as the speaker is shown to be explaining the complete meaning of the Old Testament to those entrusted with revealing its message while the vision will make that available to humanity as well.

In examining the letters, there is a clear allusion to the Old Testament in four of them which points toward the stages of Judaism prior to the public life of Jesus. Ephesus has a comment on "before you fell" and on "the tree of life set in God's paradise." They sound like language from just after the time of the Garden of Eden story. Pergamum has a sentence about Balaam and Balak and Israelites eating food from pagan sacrifices. This story from chapters 22-25 of Numbers would relate to the desert experience after the Exodus event. The letter ends with a comment on "manna" which is also related to the desert time. Thyatira includes a significant comment on Jezebel which relates to the northern kingdom of Israel after the Israelites had control of Palestine. Finally, Laodicea has the Messiah "standing at a door knocking" which would be Judaism just prior to Jesus' public life. With those four giving an indication of the stages of Jewish development, a similar meaning can be suggested for the other three cities, even though that is not clear without the clues of the first four. Smyrna would describe the time between the early Genesis account and the desert, so it would fit the time when Israel was enslaved in Egypt. Sardis would be the time of exile in Babylon when, perhaps, the Israelites thought the covenant relationship was dead and acted accordingly. Philadelphia would represent the time after the exile when the Jews lived in Palestine under foreign domination. The switch of places for the statement "listen to what the Spirit is saying" and "to those who prove victorious" at the fourth city would occur when the Israelites settled in the promised land and constructed the temple. So the change of phrases occurs after a turning point in Israel's acceptance of the gift of land from God, also pointing somewhat to this type of understanding of the letters.

The letter to Ephesus would be the starting point for the Jewish understanding of life separated from God after the original fall. The speaker is the creator (2:1, Jn 1:1) who has all of the angels to do his will (in his right hand) and intended human life in creation to surround him by being present in the churches. He knows all about creation (2:2) and knows that life on earth is difficult and close to evil. Those who have responded to God (2:3) are the ones who shun the wicked and those with false religions. The complaint against these followers (2:4) is that the love they showed in the original garden when they were surrounded with God's love has now left them. Unless they change back to loving people (2:5), they will not reflect God's love and will lose their relationship with God (church). They don't follow the practice of Nicolaitans (2:6), but there is no real indication of what that term means so it is difficult to interpret. Interpretations proposed in commentaries for the term Nicolaitans have the appearance of a guess made by the commentators based only on what is in the letters rather than any real knowledge of the term. A more interesting proposal is that the name could be stated as "nika laon" with the meaning of "he conquered the people."[14] That title would refer to the dragon who is described as "making war" on that remnant of humanity who "obey God's commandments" (12:17). The other people on earth would be considered conquered and accepting the authority of evil or of "nika laon." The closing promise (2:7) of being fed "from the tree of life set in God's paradise" reinforces the original fall meaning. It also introduces a meaning, that will become clear later, that the living relationship with God would have become available in the plan of God if evil had been successfully repulsed in Eden (12:5).

The letter to Smyrna would relate to the Israelites who were slaves in Egypt prior to the Exodus. The speaker is identified as one "who was dead and has come back to life" (2:8) and that would speak to the Israelite's position as slaves who would not be released. They have had trials and seem poor (2:9) but they have the richness of being the only people with a relationship with the True God. There are others, the Egyptians, who claim to have a relationship with gods but that is false and a response to Satan, or, as will be seen in the vision, to the dragon.

There was an ordeal of ten plagues in Egypt which could be called "ten days" (2:10) of strife and a conclusion that some of them may die, but it is the opening to real life. However, "ten days" simply means that fullness of days or a lifetime, and there was a period of slavery that came to an end after a generation had passed or when the next phase of God's calling had occurred. The generation would be the eighty years from Moses' birth until the Israelites left Egypt in the Exodus (Dt 34:7). The ones who succeed (2:11) will not have to worry about a final judgment as a "second death" since they would be open to a life which never ends.

The letter to Pergamum would fit the situation of the desert experience after the Exodus. Here the speaker (2:12) is the one with the sharp, double-edged sword (coming from his mouth, 1:16), which is the revelation of the Law which occurred in the desert. The place where Satan is enthroned (2:13) would be the desert because it seems to be a waterless place without life, which in such early times would indicate an absence of divinity and, therefore, the haunt of evil (18:2). A common interpretation in commentaries would point out that a pagan shrine with a great altar was excavated at Pergamum over a century ago, with the altar being shipped to a museum in Berlin, and that must be the meaning of the "Satan is enthroned" statement. However, the Israelites built their faith in the desert ordeal when God was with them but not expected to be present, so the desert experience fits the test better than the archeological find of the altar. The Balaam and Balak story (2:14) is a reasonably clear description of what happened to the Israelites at the end of the desert period (Num 22:2-25:18) to further the tie to the desert period. Here the Nicolaitans are mentioned again (2:15) and, because it comes after "eating food that had been sacrificed to idols," that interpretation as the meaning of the term is often given in commentaries. Yet, there is a distinction made that others who are as bad as the ones involved in pagan sacrifices "accept what the Nicolaitans teach." If those eating food from pagan sacrifices were the meaning of Nicolaitan, the two groups would be combined rather than being separated by the distinction. Then in the next section (2:20) where eating food sacrificed to idols is charged as a sin of the people, there is no mention of Nicolaitans, so the name is unlikely to mean the ones practicing that particular sin. Repentance must come from those who leave the desert or revelation (the sword out of the mouth) (2:16) will be used to condemn them. For the victorious (2:17), however, there will be bread from heaven, as was given in the desert, and unblemished stones, perhaps with the name of the tribes written on them (Ex 28:9-14) or the name that replaces the tribal covenant name.

The letter to Thyatira has very specific ties to the northern kingdom at the time of the kings when, even though split into two kingdoms, Israel was near the totality of its power. The speaker as one with "eyes like a burning flame" (2:18) would indicate that he could see that the Israelites, even with their success, were moving away from the covenant. While there are positive statements about charity, faith, devotions, and progress amidst difficulties (2:19), following Jezebel and her teaching about false sacrifices was not acceptable (2:20). Without reform she will die (2:21-22) and, without repentance, all her children as well (2:23). Since all the Israelites of the northern kingdom were moved to oblivion by the Assyrians, it fits the Jezebel situation better than just the use of her name. The churches, communities of God, would recognize that judgment will come from what is in people's hearts and on "what their behavior deserves" (2:23). Perhaps the southern kingdom (2:24), which had not been open to worship away from the temple, needed to remain loyal to their traditions in worship to receive the promised Messiah. The victorious (2:25-28) will have authority over the "nations," which represents a Greek word often translated as "Gentiles." The translator switches to "nations" to fit the late date of the traditional context. The victorious also will have the Morning Star to rule over the world (the one who brings the Day of the Lord) (Am 5:18-20), rather than only over Palestine. God has given such authority to his Messiah who would destroy human political kingdoms as one could shatter an earthenware pot. Like each of the last four letters, this ends with the advice

to listen to the Spirit (2:29) after the statement on being victorious rather than before it.

CHAPTER 3

The letter to Sardis seems to reflect the time of the Exile
and its uncertainties for Judaism. The speaker has not only the
completeness of the churches, but the completeness of the Spirit
of God to bring everlasting life to humanity (3:1). A remnant
that have died to their previous lives are called to wake up (3:2),
to revive themselves with new life. It is a call reflected in
Ezekiel's prophesies of life even for dry bones (Ez 37:1-14). They
should return to what they were in their first calling when the
covenant was their only life. If they fail to come to a new life,
judgment will be sudden and unexpected (3:3) which probably
means they will have walked away from the covenant and
judged themselves. Some who were forced to endure the Exile
were innocent (3:4) and those who accept a new life will have
their names remain in the book of life (3:5). The speaker will
remember them before the Father and his angels, just as Jesus
promised to his disciples (Mk 8:38).

The letter to Philadelphia would be the times after the
Exile when Judaism was under foreign control. The speaker has
the key of the Messiah (3:7) but what is opened at this time in
Judaism is the knowledge that Yahweh is the only God of all creation. Once that is known, there could never be a return to the
polytheism that can exist with pagan gods. So, even if they are
not strong enough to rule their own land, they have a spiritual
strength that can never be closed down again. Judaism would
have its historical view of the kingdom, but what occurs will be
God's choice (3:8) and no one can choose another or revoke
God's plan. The speaker knows their fidelity to the commandments and they will be kept safe even in trials for the world
(3:9-10) and the destruction of those who falsely claim to worship the True God. This could apply to any worship other than
Judaism, but may be directed specifically at the situation of
Daniel's time (167-164 BC) when a pagan statue was placed in
the temple and caused the Maccabee's revolt. Some Jews also

supported the establishment of Greek culture in Judah at that time. However, the future trial "for the whole world" doesn't sound like a persecution only for Christians and Jews, but a decision that would be made at the last judgment time. The faithful (3:12) will be the supports for the new sanctuary of God and the new Jerusalem. They shall be given the name of God and the name of the Messiah, perhaps in the sealing shown in the vision.

The letter to Laodicia would represent Judaism at the time of the Messiah's proclamation. The speaker (3:14), called "the faithful, the true witness, the ultimate source of God's creation," brings a message to those who think Judaism of the first century is the end point of the kingdom, and the message is that the true kingdom greatly exceeds that expectation. If they are lukewarm to the full message (3:15-16), the Messiah will vomit them out of His life. They believe themselves rich because of the ancient covenant (3:17), but without the new life they are poor, blind and naked with respect to what God wants them to have. There are no clothes with meaning next to the white robe of the new Jerusalem (3:18). The famous eye ointment from Laodicia may heal eyes, but the Anointing of the Messiah brings light into life "to see" in a way not otherwise possible. Jesus then claims to be the one who disciplines (3:19) and calls them to repent even though the quote would say God disciplines (Pr 3:11-12). The time has come, the Messiah knocks (3:20) and whoever invites him into their lives welcomes true life into themselves. The meal would mean a great closeness to Judaism, but ultimately it could be a reference to the Eucharist even though not understandable at the time of the vision. The victorious (3:21) will be brought into the life with God.

In summary, letters one, three, four and seven include information that ties in quite clearly with the times of the Jewish salvation history indicated in the analysis. The other three letters would not be so clear in themselves but once the pattern is established, they fit well into their assigned places. It would seem that the person writing the Book is indicating that some background is needed before one can address the great visions starting in chapter four. This would be a way of saying some-

thing about the necessity of knowing the whole record of revelation up to the point of this writing even though it is not the type
of completeness that is found in the vision recorded in this
Book. If the vision was opened to just anyone, the understanding might be so limited as to be indescribable. For a Jew enough
would be understood to proclaim the message. However, the
vision is not only for Judaism, and hence the background is
placed in a non-Jewish setting of the place intended for the
translation of the writing.

The vision is the Revelation about Jesus Christ; He is the
whole focus of the writing. He is the revelation itself. Placing
the seven letters before the opening of the vision of the revelation has no meaning if they are intended to be just letters. There
is no connection with those cities before the revelation. However, if those seven letters are a summary of the stages of development of the plan of God to Judaism, they do precede Jesus. No
matter how artificial they might seem, they are the pertinent
introduction. Placed in a Gentile setting would only be a way of
stating the obvious, that the revelation to Judaism was never
meant only for Judaism but for all people. Even if written later as
an introduction to the description of the vision, they belong and
find their meaning in the beginning of the Book.

Therefore, a summary that tied into the communities of
the Roman Province of Asia would be perfect for the message
being delivered to those communities. The letters become the
introduction for the opening of the plan of God which will
reveal Jesus as the Lamb that is to bring to fruition the salvation
of the world as planned by God from the beginning. There is
nothing to indicate that they are a vision to the original John
anymore than the introduction, with its strong connection to
Jesus, was written by John the Baptist. Yes, the message (vision)
originally comes to John the Baptist but he isn't necessarily the
one who prepares this composition. The orders to him to "write
down" means to proclaim, to make known to everyone and the
Book would be an essential step in that process when John is
prevented from further activity.

CHAPTER 4 - The Great Vision

The abruptness of the opening of the vision is well stated by John, sitting on a rock in the sun we might think, and suddenly he can see into heaven. It is a new vision filled with Old Testament images or described in such images. The immediate center of the vision is "One who was sitting on the throne" (4:2) from Isaiah's initial calling (Is 6:1) but, in the reverence of this vision, the Divine name is not stated.

The appearance of the One on the throne was of Jasper and Carnelian (4:3) which are the stones in the priest's breastpiece for Benjamin and Ruben, the youngest and the oldest of the sons of Jacob (Ex 28:17-21).[15] Perhaps the meaning only has to do with the last and the first in the way stated, but is more likely to represent all of the tribes. The rainbow would be the symbol of the covenant (Gen 9:12-17), however, here it looked like an emerald, the stone signifying Judah. It doesn't mean the rainbow is entirely green but that Judah was the only tribe remaining, other than fragments of the others, so the covenant would look like Judah in an early context for the vision.

The twenty-four elders sitting on a circle of thrones (4:4) represent double the fullness of Israel. The meaning of twenty-four would seem to come from two groups in Judaism who would represent its fullness. That could be the priests who secure the covenant relationship in carrying out the requirements of the Law and the prophets who judge Israel's living out of the covenant (Jer 33:17-23). This meaning would fit the repetition of "a line of kings and priests" used elsewhere in the Book (1:6, 5:10) and also stand for the Law and the prophets. The twelve tribes and the kings exist for only part of the time of Israel. However, prophets in Jewish terms include leaders as former prophets and written prophets as later prophets. The offering of sacrifices starts with Abraham so that would make priesthood an entity from the start even though the divine mandate would start with Aaron. At the time of John the Baptist, Judaism would only consider the Law and the Prophets as a canon of the Jewish Scriptures. Additional writings that may have been kept among the scrolls in the synagogues would be referred to as the "writings" but were not considered as part of the canon of Scripture until the Council of Jamnia after the year 70. Those writings included books that later were not included in the Jewish canon and probably included some not included in the Christian Old Testament. However, by the end of the first century some of those extra books would have been included in the Jewish Scriptures as a result of decisions made at the Jewish Council of Jamnia. The Law and Prophets, or priests and kings as used here, would be an accurate understanding of the twenty-four elders and also be an indication that the description of the visions would be earlier than the decision of Jamnia.

The term elders in Judaism of the first century is related to synagogue leaders which is not consistent with priests, for sure, and, possibly, not for prophets. However, elder carries the meaning of one who is wise due to many years. That is usually seen as the reason for giving very long ages to persons who were great in Israel. So it could be a title applicable to everyone who had been holy or close to God.

The thunder and lightning is a traditional description of the presence of God called a theophany (4:5). The "seven Spirits" of God would mean the completeness of God's Spirit of life which becomes Holy Spirit as a name only in Christian times. The sea was such a restless body that it was believed that only God could control the sea (4:6). To have a sea that seemed like glass is the symbol that there is a total response to God in heaven. The four animals (4:6-7) represent the four basic elements of creation, the lion for fire, the bull or ox for earth, the man for water (the water carrier) and the eagle for air. Creation is shown as worshiping the glory of God even if that wasn't the view on earth at the time (4:9). The double fullness of Judaism worshiped God continuously as well (4:10-11).

CHAPTER 5

Chapter five opens by noting the scroll with the seven seals in the right hand of the One sitting on the throne. Written on both sides would mean that nothing could be added so it says the plan is complete and will remain as it is. Papyrus was normally written only on the side where the grain of the reeds was horizontal, but a scroll in heaven would be as perfect as parchment and written on both sides. The seals could indicate it is completely sealed or, since a seal validated a document, it was completely validated or, as a plan of God, it was a complete plan (Eph 3:10-11). All three are probably true since the plan can only be opened by one who is worthy to do God's work. John recognizes that no one seems to be available who is worthy, but an elder points out that the Lamb is the Messiah who has triumphed and will open the scroll (5:5). Normally, we would think that the triumph of the Messiah, when the Lamb was slain, would be after the time of John the Baptist, but the plan covers all of creation, so what occurs in the vision includes past, present and future events. However, while the image of the Lamb is meaningful prior to the coming of Jesus, it would not seem to be appropriate at the end of the first century when Christ's sacrifice was both known and discussed and regularly celebrated by the church.

The Lamb stands between the four animals and the twenty-four elders (5:6) or on the creation side of the throne and as an intermediary to Judaism. He "seemed to have been sacrificed" (literally "as having been slain") which indicates he has been an acceptable sacrifice in a very special way since the body in addition to the life has come to heaven. A normal sacrifice would have the life leave the victim in the blood which was then poured on the altar or around its base. The life belonging to God would come to God while the body remained on earth. Since the Lamb is alive, the description is of a victim resurrected and in heaven. If the Lamb has triumphed in being an acceptable or worthy sacrifice, the Lamb is the Messiah who is worthy to bring judgment and salvation to the world. The seven horns would mean complete power and the seven eyes would mean complete wisdom or, as stated here, the eyes are the seven Spirits so they represent wisdom that comes from God and is sent throughout creation.

The Lamb takes the scroll from the right hand of God and a distinct change occurs in heaven (4:7-14). The four animals representing creation which had been glorifying and honoring the One on the throne (4:9) now prostrate themselves before the Lamb (5:8). The twenty-four elders who had prostrated themselves to worship the One on the throne (4:10) also switch to prostrating themselves before the Lamb. They then sing a new song which means a complete change in their praise, now directed to the Lamb also. This new song is then echoed by a song of praise from all the angels of heaven with the sevenfold attributes of the Lamb reflecting the completeness of the praise (5:11-12) in addition to the completeness of the attributes. Finally, praise comes from all the creatures of earth, in the air, on the earth, underneath the earth (possibly Sheol) and in the sea (5:13). The development from those witnessing the opening, to those throughout heaven, and to those existing on earth follows the progression of seals, trumpets, and bowls for the contents of the plan of God.

CHAPTER 6 - Seven Seals

The opening of the seals in chapter six starts with a release of horses and riders, a symbol of strength that is very fast and difficult to stop or even evade. The first seal reveals a white horse, which in Revelation is a color related to that which is close to God. The rider (6:2) is not identified but holds a bow as a covenant symbol; he wears a victory crown and goes from victory to victory. The thunder with his entrance could indicate the presence of God at the start or a union between God and humanity as the first meaning in the plan of God. Since the white horse will return later (19:11-16) with the King of Kings as the rider, this initial rider would represent an initial union of God with humanity before the fall which should have been the start of the covenant relationship. The intervention of evil at the start prevented the covenant from being completed (12:4-6), so this initial rider "went away" from creation. The victories of the rider would occur wherever human minds are opened to the plan of God in dramatic events, such as the Exodus, or in the slow and mysterious awareness that there is only One God for all of creation. The culminating victory is his death and resurrection. While not stated, the disappearance of the planned relationship between God and humanity may have resulted in the appearance of three horses, red, black and pale green reflecting war, famine and plague being released upon earth. They represent conditions in a creation where the human element has severed the direct connection to God intended in creation.

The rider of the red horse from the second seal (6:3-4) has as his duty to take away peace and has a huge sword to carry out his duty. The black horse of the third seal (6:5-6) represents famine and has a rider who will sell food when a famine eliminated local crops. A "days wages" would be required to feed one person with wheat and only three people with barley which is less affected by conditions causing famine. The pale green horse of the fourth seal (6:7-8) is identified by the rider's name "plague" and was followed closely by Sheol, the place of the dead.

Each horse and rider is called out by one of the four animals grouped around the throne. The first call would have been the lion representing fire if the order is retained from the earlier description (4:7). Fire or specifically lightning would be accompanied by thunder which calls out the first horse and together they are the common expression of a theophany. However, in the Old Testament fire often carries the meaning of the presence of God as in the burning bush (Ex 3:1-6) and the pillar of fire (Nu 14:14) which is repeated in this Book (10:1). So the presence of God in creation is strongly supported as a concept that exists in God's plan from the beginning and is so indicated in the Old Testament record. This surely would be interpreted as the part of the plan called forth by God. However, it is not shown in the trumpets or bowls so it must come only in revelation rather than proclaimed and made clear from nature as was intended in the plan.

The remaining three horses represent part of nature on earth when the heavenly garden is not the situation of humanity due to evil. The red horse would be called forth with a shout from the ox representing earth which is the sphere of war once earth has been made devoid of peace. The black horse representing famine would be called out by the human face representing water. Rainfall left without the control of God as in the garden would be sufficiently intermittent that its lack at times would cause reoccurring famine. The fourth horse and rider would be called forth by the eagle representing air. The uncontrolled spread of plague could be seen as having air as its vehicle even at that early time.

The final three horses come from the nature of creation. They may reflect the different conditions of initial humanity when leaving the garden (Gen 3:16-19 and Rev 12:13-17) but not in the specific wording. They are derived more clearly from the prophecy of Ezekiel as a result of sinfulness (Ez 14:12-23), however, without the wild beasts unless the horses were intended to bring in that element. The red horse of warfare is the opposite of God and the peace of Eden. The black horse of want is the opposite of God's intention in providing a garden for humanity. The pale green horse of plagues and death was not intended by God in the garden but became a condition resulting from leaving the garden. If the union with God had been retained at the start, there would have been no need for what followed. They are the result of allowing evil to intervene. The three could be seen as conditions created to show humanity that to return to the relationship with God was the obvious choice for happiness. The question of afterlife was examined in the wisdom literature of late Judaism and, by about the time of the birth of the Messiah, brought a conclusion that there would be an afterlife for those who responded to God. So the language of the four horsemen is not something totally unknown to Judaism but would be recognized as an answer to their speculations in the wisdom period.

The fifth seal introduces the souls of holy people who died because of their witness to the revelation from God (6:9-11). Prior to Jesus' death and Resurrection, the dead would go to Sheol to wait for whatever afterlife would be given. However, those who had been holy and who died because of their witness would deserve life in heaven according to the plan of God. They would be an acceptable sacrifice to God, but with the plan not fully opened, heaven would not be open to them as yet. However, they would have the white robes that guaranteed salvation and would have to wait for the victory of the Lamb over evil which would come in the Resurrection. They wait underneath the altar because their sacrifice is acceptable even if not yet fulfilled. When their blood (life) has been mixed with the blood (life) of the Lamb, heaven will be opened for all (7:14, 20:4-5).

The sixth seal reveals the Great Day of Yahweh which Judaism saw as the completion of God's kingdom on earth and their time of peace and freedom (6:12-17). However, there were warnings (Amos 5:18-20) that the Great Day might bring great misery on those not deserving of the blessings of God regardless of their positions in life (Jer 7:1-20). The description opened in this seal is an end-of-creation scene, not the creation of a place for Judaism on earth as the Day of the Lord had been seen. Even the privileged people with wealth and power on earth (6:15), who perhaps could escape the effects of the last three horsemen, wars, famine and plagues, will be involved in the destruction at the end of creation. Those who deserve punishment will wish for a natural disaster to end their existence rather than allowing them to face the judgment they will receive on that day or perhaps its eternal result. The language that includes comments about the "anger of the lamb" and God's anger (6:17) might be acceptable prior to the coming of the Messiah, but would be in disagreement with the end of the New Testament revelation about God's love (1 Jn 4:16). Anger would reflect separation that exists when there is no relationship, which here would mean the Old Testament covenant. Those who face the judgment without a relationship with God would not want to face the decision they had made.

CHAPTER 7 - Interlude to the Seals

An interlude in the events related to the opening of the seals (7:1-17) occurs in which four angels hold back the judgment until the servants of God are sealed. Everyone has the opportunity to make a choice between God as the Lord govern-

ing one's life or to choose an association with some power in creation. The "angel rising where the sun rises" (7:2) is the
Morning Star which will bring the Day of the Lord, but here
would be the Messiah who delays that event to allow a choice to
be made and witnessed to the world. This choice scene will be
repeated in the sixth of the trumpets (9:13-23) and bowls
(16:12-16) and in the sixth of the final unnumbered visions
(20:7-10).

The response among the people of Israel (7:4-8) is a
combination of twelve from each tribe, the number that would
indicate they are followers of Israel, times 1,000 which is a great
number but not completely defined. Taken as an absolute number of 144,000, it would be a small percentage of all the
Israelite/Jewish people. However, taken in terms of the meaning
of the numbers twelve as Judaism and one thousand, meaning a
large undefined number, the result would be a great number of
Jewish people from each tribe.

Then John is shown "a huge number, impossible to
count, from every nation, race, tribe and language" who were
also counted among the saved (7:9-12). They would be Gentiles
who had been saved through the Lamb with the coming of the
Messiah. Their shouts are praise for the victory of God and the
Lamb. This would be the future situation at the time of the last
judgment, but representing the cumulative result of the whole
time of creation. However, the angels who were standing around
the throne (and around the elders and the four animals or with
them) worshiped God but the Lamb is not mentioned, unlike
the response when the Lamb took the sealed scroll from the One
on the throne (5:11-14). It would seem that the understanding
of the Lamb by John is not as clear at the time just before the
opening of the final seal as it was when the fully sealed plan was
accepted by the Lamb from God.

The elder offers an explanation of the multitudes
(7:13-17) as those who had been through the "great affliction"
(or translated as tribulation and as persecution according to the
beliefs of the translator) and who "have washed their robes white
again in the blood of the Lamb." These multitudes are in heav-

en so it would seem that the last judgment would be the "great affliction" rather than a persecution by Domitian or any other Roman emperor. In the temple sacrifice the priests would draw the blood (the life) which belongs to God from the animal and offer it on the altar (Ex 24:7) or pour it at the base of the altar (Ex 29:12). Since life belonged to God, this gift would be acceptable to God. The carcass could be burned in a holocaust but primarily it would remain to be consumed by the one giving the sacrifice with portions given to those serving in the temple. If blood got on a priest's white garment, the spot would have to be washed out immediately. The need for immediate action could be seen as necessary to prevent a stain from becoming permanent. However, the most important ritual need of the sacrifice would be that no part of what was a gift to God could be removed from the altar area of the temple and lost in a later washing process. The gift to God is the life of the animal and no part of the gift can go elsewhere.

This description gives an opposite opinion because the sacrifice of the Lamb of God was for the salvation of the multitudes. The blood of the Lamb (or the life of Christ) was meant to be the means of saving humans. The blood (life of Christ) must be on each person in order for them to enter heaven. Putting on and living the life of Christ makes a disciple one with Christ. Christians accept this life of Christ, body and blood, first in baptism and again in each Eucharist as a constant renewal of their decision to make His life their own and it is the only sacrifice that matters.

In the sacrifice seen as acceptance by the Israelites of the covenant of the Law (Ex 24:3-8) half of the blood (life which belonged to God) was sprinkled on the people to produce a covenant in life. Therefore, the washing of the lives of the multitude with the life of Christ made them part of the gift acceptable to God since putting on the life of Christ meant salvation rather than a ritual concern in an animal sacrifice. The life of Christ was what truly belonged to God rather than the life of animals from earth. Those receiving it became the people who are constantly in the presence of God and are in the tent of heaven rather than at a stone temple on earth. Paul has a comment about Jews and pagans being redeemed in Christ Jesus (Rom 3:23-25) which could come from a knowledge of the scene in chapter seven, but not vice versa, pointing to an early context of the vision.

The opening of the final seal brings a silence in heaven for about a half hour (8:1). An hour for a person could mean a lifetime, so this is a half of a lifetime or about 30 years. That is given as the age of Jesus when he started his public life (Lk 3:23) so it could have the meaning that the Messiah would come into the world as the final stage of Revelation but the victory for which he is praised (7:10) would come from the death and resurrection about a half a lifetime after his birth. Everything had been started on the final stage in the incarnation but the conclusion hadn't been reached in human time. John doesn't seem to know about the incarnation of Jesus (Jn 1:31) so if that coming to earth is the "half hour" prior to the coming of Jesus there is nothing to write about concerning the seventh seal. More likely, the half hour of silence prevents John from writing about the fullness of the revelation which will be revealed by Jesus (10:4). What could remain hidden from John at the end of the first century when the revelation is complete?

CHAPTER 8 - Seven Trumpets

The seven trumpets are an announcement of the plan of God in heaven and on earth. Nothing really happened with the trumpets as nothing happened when the seals were opened. Part of the plan of God had already occurred on earth but would not be easily recognized or understood. Obviously, the fact of creation would be recognized even if pagan religions would never see the greatness of One God and the meaning of such a gift. The Jewish history was built on earlier direct revelation but that had not been fully shared with all peoples. Only as revelation is given completely will the whole meaning become known and will salvation become fully available. The plan opened and being proclaimed contains the essential completeness that goes far beyond even Jewish expectations of only an earthly kingdom for themselves in Palestine.

The first four trumpets announce what came in the first four seals (8:6-12). In the first seal the one who was to gain the covenant in life for all humanity disappears. The presence of God is not shown directly in nature but comes in revelation to Israel. Therefore, there is no protection on earth and the effects of the next three seals are proclaimed just as the four animals from around the throne called them forth. The troubles probably should be seen as natural calamities. The result of the first trumpet is troubles on land, the second affects the sea, the third affects the rivers and springs and the fourth affects the heavens. In the four, they represent all of the natural troubles on earth. The troubles are not total destruction but cause severe difficulties, here described as the loss of a third of each part of creation that was affected. These are problems, such as earthquakes, storms, floods and disease, known to creation because they have been occurring since the original fall.

An eagle then announces triple trouble for all people at the sound of the next three trumpets (8:13). If the first four trumpets announced problems in creation resulting from natural causes, this special warning of troubles would encompass problems beyond natural problems which would occur due to evil. An eagle as a symbol in Scripture tends to be an agent of Yahweh. The Israelites are said to be carried to safety on eagle's wings (Ex 19:4) just as the woman in creation in this Book (12:14). Yahweh is compared to an eagle (Dt 32:11) who spreads his wings to save Jacob. The wings of the eagle might be seen as the Law and the prophets, which together act as agents of Yahweh and which protect Israel from a false choice of pagan religions. It isn't the natural problems on earth that would be described as a trouble, but something that requires special attention. Therefore, this particular use of the eagle image may mean only a warning.

CHAPTER 9

With the fifth trumpet evil is introduced as a trouble and the sixth trumpet has a judgment aspect which seems to indicate there would be an intervention of revelation for Israel to choose wisely. The Law and the prophets would be necessary to recognize the Messiah, which is why revelation would come through Judaism. So this warning of trouble would relate to something far beyond natural disasters brought on from the original fall as in the first four trumpets. As a guide Israel would need revelation to remain faithful to Yahweh. Without such guidance, they would not recognize evil and may accept it as the Gentiles would have done. A reading of the Song of Moses and his warning to the Israelites (Dt 32:1-47) tends to fit very well with what is faced following the first four trumpets. Some of the images of the song reflect the first four trumpets (Dt 32:21-22) with a fire "blazed out" from God's anger that devours the earth and its produce (first trumpet) and setting fire to the foundations of the mountain (second trumpet). That Yahweh would rouse the Israelites to jealousy with what is "no people" (Dt 32:21) reflects the salvation of the uncountable multitudes which seem to be Gentiles (7:9).

The fifth trumpet, with the star that had fallen from heaven (9:1), is Satan hurled down from heaven by Michael which is described later as trouble coming to earth (12:7-12). Satan can open the shaft to the abyss which would be outside of inhabited creation and bring evil into creation. Such evil would not kill or harm creation (9:5), but would cause much pain to people as it always does (Wis 11:15-20). However, that pain could only come to those without "God's seal on their foreheads" (Lk 10:17-19). For those who put all their hopes in what they have on earth, it would be difficult to cope with adversity. What seems attractive at first turns into teeth that can harm in the end (9:7-8). Those who have God's seal on their foreheads have put their hope in that relationship and have given away this life. They will witness to what is eternally important even if they lose their part in this world and their very life on earth. They cannot be induced to value the riches of the world or appeal to the evil one for protection, since their trust is in the Almighty and their hope is in the everlasting life. "If they experienced punishment as men see it, their hope was rich with immortality; slight was their affliction, great will their blessing be" (Wis 3:1-9). This coming of evil produces a focus only on the world and is the first "woe" to all of creation and is different from what is actually natural.

The sixth trumpet brings the armies of world leaders in league with evil. War is part of a creation where love is not inherent in the leaders and populations. It is not something beyond the control of God, but part of the plan where peace is not sought out as a goal. The horses (9:17), whose riders have breast plates that are flame colored, hyacinth blue and sulphur yellow, are direct reflections of the red, black (hyacinth blue is very dark), and pale colored horses released in the seals (6:3-8). The armies of war are always accompanied by bloodshed, famine and plague. Since they cause such punishments among the nations it would seem that "Hades followed at their heels" (6:8). If the witness of those in a covenant with God were recognized, those subject to harm would turn to God as their protector and be spared. However, the destruction caused by war and conflict always seems to be answered by additional war and conflict. This represents the result in life even for those that historically might have escaped destruction (9:20), but whose reliance was on false religions and sacrifices and an increase in evil leadership with no giving up of "murdering or witchcraft or fornication or stealing" (9:21). The result of the sixth of each series of seven is a condition that develops on earth when evil, originally thrown out of heaven, gains allies by promoting hatred and a reliance on weapons and destruction.

CHAPTER 10 - Interlude to the Trumpets

Chapter ten opens an interlude which reflects the interlude between the sixth and seventh seals, but with greater detail. In the interlude is a scene in which an angel (10:1) of immense power and size comes wrapped in a cloud (Dn 7:13) and his face was like the sun (1:16). This would seem to be the angel with a powerful voice who opened the interlude before the seventh seal (7:2). His legs were like pillars of fire (reminding one of Ex 13:21 but are more clearly from Nu 14:14), one on land and one in the sea as if controlling both land and sea. He had a rainbow over his head (the sign of the covenant) (4:3) and in his hand a small scroll, unrolled and, therefore, already proclaimed. His face being "like the sun" is the same as the person who told John to write a book (1:16). When he spoke, there were seven claps of thunder. This would be the same voice of thunder that called forth the presence of God in creation (6:1) and with seven thunderclaps would mean the completeness of the revelation which would be the Gospel. The "powerful angel" with a voice "like a lion roaring" (10:3) and the symbol of fire (10:1) indicates involvement of the presence of God. The identity of the "angel" would be recognized by Christians at the end of the first century as being the Messiah, and the "seven thunderclaps" as being the Gospel message. The same could be said of "God's secret intention" (10:7) (or "the mysterious plan of God")[16], so this section also points toward the accuracy of using the early context for this Book rather than the traditional context at the end of the first century.

John was told he should not write down the seven thunderclaps as they should be kept secret (10:4). The scene is one in which a far greater covenant between God and humanity is to be established with the size of the messenger giving its importance. The small scroll unrolled (10:2) is the Old Testament record of revelation from the original covenant. The thunderclaps (10:4) that describe the new covenant illustrate both its importance as a new revelation and that it will be proclaimed far beyond the area of Palestine which had been home to the original revelation. John will not "write down" (proclaim) this revelation since it will be proclaimed by the Lamb. The quietness of the seventh seal (8:1) would have been the same holding back of the completeness of the plan from John. The description of the angel's oath (10:5-7) to God comes from the atonement ceremony in the time of Nehemiah (Ne 9:5-37) in which the Jewish people, then back in their own land, even though powerless, confessed their sins and transgressions. It is in direct opposition to what has been said of those who escaped the plagues in the sixth trumpet (9:20-21). With the last trumpet God's secret intention will be fulfilled (10:7).

The ending of this scene is the action where John is told to eat the small scroll (10:9). It is a small scroll because it is a small reflection of the whole plan of God. John is told it will taste sweet in his mouth but will turn his stomach sour and that occurs. The prophet Ezekiel had to eat the scroll and taste its sweetness before announcing the more difficult measures being given to the Israelites (Ez 2:9-3:3). The Old Testament revelation was very sweet at first with the Exodus event giving them freedom, the conquest gave them a land and the fulfillment in King David's time came when the conquest was completed and the temple constructed under Solomon. Yet later, when the northern kingdom was lost completely, they saw a great setback, since the majority of the people, the land and their wealth were lost. Two centuries later the people of the southern kingdom went into exile in Babylon for almost the remaining lifetime of all the adults who were exiled. Finally Judaism returned and lived in their land, but it always remained under the rule of foreigners. This second half of their history was a time which could be compared with a sour stomach and it was not understood. The eating of the scroll, which is a taking in of the existing revelation, is a requirement for understanding the whole plan of God, similar to what has been proposed above for the seven letters. After that experience John is told he must prophesy again on a much grander scale than has ever occurred before in Israel (10:11), speaking about different "nations and countries and languages and emperors." The vision has expressed this expanded audience earlier (5:9, 7:9), but at this point the prophet is told he must make clear that the revelation to come must be proclaimed beyond Judaism to the whole world.

CHAPTER 11

This description of the Great City shows most clearly the effects of calling this writing apocalyptic and assuming that everything is expressed in a type of code. The city has a temple which is Jewish with only an outer court open to Gentiles so its identification would be Jerusalem (11:1-2). The measuring is a reference to chapter 40 of Ezekiel where the measuring was shown in a vision at the time the Israelites were in exile for not fulfilling the covenant requirements. The city with the temple is called a "holy city" yet only a city near God could be holy, so only Jerusalem as the place where Yahweh choose to give His name a home would be called holy (Dt 12:5), yet it doesn't exist after the year 70. The city with the temple is the place of the two witnesses, represented by Joshua the high priest and Zerubbabel an anointed leader as a kingly figure (Zech 4:3,14), who would prophesy during the time of testing. It is a reference to the Law and the prophets (or priests and prophets) found in the place of the temple. Then in what appears to be a later addition at the time of the translation, the city is defined as the place "in which their Lord was crucified," again pointing to Jerusalem (11:8). The measuring is to determine if the temple and the witnesses actually fulfilled the meaning of the revelation that had already come to the people of God.

The reading seems designed to clearly indicate that Jerusalem is the Great City and to reference Old Testament quotes to show why the city would be punished by an earthquake for its failure. The destruction of the city (17:16) would be caused by a judgment against the sacrificial worship at the temple and not a judgment against the Jewish people who will be called out of the city (18:1-8). The two witnesses had remained in the city, or only in Judaism. They appeared to be dead because they never went to the whole people of the earth and invited them into a union with the only God of creation, but left those people in a pagan relationship with idols. Yet, commentaries, by assuming that all of this writing is a code rather than the application of Old Testament allusions and quotes, define the city as Rome. That remarkable switch would not be necessary, except that the choice of a context after 70 means there is no temple in Jerusalem and hardly much of a city. So, with a variety of explanations, commentators make the city Rome even though none of the clear allusions to Jerusalem can be switched convincingly to Rome.

The temple is God's sanctuary, which in a first century writing by either Jews or Christians was the temple in Jerusalem.

A twentieth century commentator might twist the meaning to fit a pagan city for whatever purpose, but it would be a form of blasphemy for a first century writer (an inspired writer at that) to make such a statement. The witnesses could triumph over their own enemies or the enemies of the Great City if they acted as true witnesses. References to their power to control the rain and bring plagues on their enemies are historical references to such power (11:5-6). However, their time of witnessing is in the time of trial when the beast has power on earth and when their time of witness ends it will be because they will be replaced on earth by the Messiah.

The Great City is known by the names Sodom and Egypt (11:8). The prophets used Sodom as a name or comparison for Jerusalem when they judged that Israel was not fulfilling the covenant (Is 1:9-10 and 3:8-9, Jer 23:14, Ez 16:46-51, Am 4:10-11). The term Egypt was not used for Jerusalem in the Old Testament, but if religious authorities in Jerusalem prevented the covenant relationship from being opened to "every people, race, language, and nation" the name Egypt might be applied. The Israelites were enslaved in Egypt and for that time could not witness to the original covenant relationship with God. The name Egypt could apply to Jerusalem at the time of this writing because the promises meant for all people had become "enslaved" in Judaism and would not be allowed to be proclaimed throughout the world (10:11). The witnesses to the covenant relationship would appear dead to Gentiles because there would be no invitation for them to enter the covenant. Adding the reference to the crucifixion at a time when the vision was recorded or translated and given to the Christian church, rather than when first seen by John in the vision, would clarify that Jerusalem is the Great City.

At the end of the time of trial (11:11), life will be returned to the witnesses of the covenant relationship because it is going to be fulfilled (Mt 5:17-19). Christ and those who put on the life of Christ become the witnesses to the fulfillment of salvation and so the earlier witnesses are removed to heaven (11:12). An earthquake, something that shakes the Great City, occurs and the survivors praise the God of Heaven (11:13). These survivors must be the Jewish people associated with Jerusalem and the temple, since the world which is to be punished in the events of the sixth trumpet continued to worship evil beings and did not give up sinning (9:20-21). This whole section on the temple and the Great City becomes clear and convincing in the early context. All the explanations that are used to support a context at the end of the first century are an unacceptable twisting of the evidence. Later, "Babylon," as the Great City, would require the same distortion.

The fifth trumpet was the first trouble as evil was allowed to affect the earth. The sixth trumpet was the second trouble, the unleashing of the evil of the three horsemen as armies that result from evil gaining control of empires in history. The third trouble, the last that is included in the plan of God, would be the judgment that comes with the destruction of the world. Judgment and destruction of the world would follow the coming of God to earth at the end of time (11:19). That would occur with the opening of the heavens when the kingdom would be revealed as a closeness to God never seen earlier. The kingdom of the world will become the kingdom of God and his Messiah (11:15). This kingdom would be composed of those who accept the reign of God in themselves rather than an artificial area on earth. Yet the kingdom is open to everyone on earth (Ps 2:1-8). It is clear that this is a judgment time in which the dead are judged and those found to be holy are rewarded.

The seventh trumpet proclaims the judgment time which opens in the interlude of establishing the kingdom of "the Lord and his Christ" which would start with the public life of the Messiah (11:15). Later, John the Baptist will see this as a time of terrible destruction (Mt 3:7-12) and won't understand Jesus' openness to the very people who were not keeping the Law (Mt 11:2-3). However, judgment is determined by each person (Jn 5:24-30) by choosing eternal life or choosing the world. This will become clear by seeing the decision that the world makes in the expanded scenes of chapters 12 to 20. Once that decision has been made, the world will disappear and everyone will get what they have chosen. As the sanctuary of God is opening in the vision (11:19), and the presence of God is entering creation, it may not be completely clear to John the Baptist. When creation disappears so does the meaning of the kingdom of earth and only the kingdom of heaven will be left as a place to live.

CHAPTER 12 - The Woman

The vision of the woman and what occurs due to evil has been interpreted historically as a symbol of Mary or the church or Israel. It may be in some way such a symbol, but it clearly extends beyond those meanings. The woman, almost by definition, is the most important element in creation, standing on the moon and adorned by the lights of heaven. Since the earth is not included in the description, the woman seems to represent the meaning of the earth. She would represent all of humanity because, in the plan of God, all are invited to salvation. She is pregnant and ready to give birth to a male child, yet she is the source of humanity threatened by evil (12:17). The connection to Mary as a symbol is reinforced by the description of her children as those "who obey God's commandments and bear witness to Jesus" (12:17). The dragon would be opposed to that part of humanity which accepted the true God. However, if those obeying the commandments are only "the rest" of her children, others who haven't obeyed the commandments also must be her children. Therefore the woman is the mother of humanity rather than an individual person. However, she is not an Eve representation, but as humanity in the plan of God. The "twelve stars on her head for a crown" would indicate that Judaism, as the start of a covenant relationship with God, would be her crowning glory at the time of the vision. That would emphasize that she represents all of humanity and her glory comes from the relationship with God granted through revelation.

Evil, in the form of the red dragon, wishes to interfere with the coming birth, knowing it would mean human salvation through a human union with God, something evil cannot have without changing (Wis 2:23-24). Evil is powerful, the ten horns represent the fullness of power but not complete power. Evil has the completeness of knowledge (as distinct from wisdom) which is indicated by the seven heads and gives the dragon its dominance in heaven as indicated by the coronets on the heads while in heaven. Stars often represent angelic figures and the sweeping of a third of the stars from the sky could represent defections of angels to follow the red dragon.

The child would represent Christ or, in an indirect way if there were no fall of humanity, a relationship in life with God for humans. The association of humanity with the dragon, given here without the Garden of Eden story, represents the loss of the original relationship that was part of the plan of God from the beginning and which returns and remains with God. The woman then escapes to the earth and to the desert as an opposition to the garden. There is an element of safety on earth in that the dragon would operate on earth only indirectly as an evil spirit rather than through its power. The 1,260 days (12:6) in this section would be the time from the fall until the coming of the Messiah which would be a half-time of testing until salvation comes, rather than a literal number of days which would have no meaning.

The war between Michael and the dragon is a direct result of the dragon's attempt to destroy the plan of God and, thereby, to prevent the giving of a sharing of divine life with humanity. The dragon loses and is sent to earth in a loss of angelic power (9:1), but with much evil influence to be used to gain power on earth. The dragon's fall is hailed by those who describe the dragon as a persecutor (actually accuser) and who themselves accepted martyrdom rather than a relationship with evil (12:10-12). Their triumph is attributed to the blood of the Lamb even though Jesus would not have been crucified by this time so the sacrifice is in the eternal plan of God and is only seen on earth at the time of the crucifixion. This would explain the birth of the male child by the woman as inherent in the union of divine and human life as God's gift known at the time of creation but not seen in the revelation on earth until a later time.

The pursuit of the dragon after the woman (12:13) on

earth is the continuing goal of evil to prevent humanity from sharing God's life. The wings of the eagle (12:14) would be the Law and the prophets which give knowledge of evil and of the covenant relationship which allows humanity to find safety (Ex 19:4). The water from the evil one (12:15) now on earth reflects the Exodus event which is obstructed by the earth, or by creation in general which follows the plan of God (Wis 19:6-8). The evil one then makes war on the children of the woman who follow the commandments (12:17). This would mean that the woman represents Israel on earth as the relationship with God even though the relationship would be open to all of humanity.

The term desert has particular meaning to Judaism which is important to the references in this Book. In Jewish tradition a desert would seem to be a place without the presence of God because there is no rainfall, something that would come with the presence of God. The original fear of the Israelites when they left the scene of the Exodus event, where the presence of God was so clear in protecting them, was the question of who would protect them in the wilderness (or desert) or how would they be fed (Ps 78:17-20). Later, the desert would be seen as a place of evil, but not because evil was in the desert, but because God's presence would not be in the desert except after the Exodus during the time of wandering. Here the description of the Law and prophets (12:6 and 12:13-14) is noted to show that the covenant relationship was given to maintain a relationship with God even when it would appear, at least from a lack of rainfall, that God wasn't present. There is a mixing of the "desert" and "earth" in general. Later in chapter 17, the harlot on the scarlet beast will choose to stay in the "desert" rather than respond to the coming of the kingdom of God and will meet destruction. As the kingdom of God moves beyond the temple worship of Judaism, the presence of God moves beyond only a single part of creation.

CHAPTER 13 - Sea Beast and False Prophet

The beast from the sea is an embodiment of the evil dragon, now on earth (13:1), but forced to rule through leading human forces astray. Emerging from the sea would mean coming from the abyss or from outside of creation, perhaps part of the unlocking of the abyss noted in the fifth trumpet (9:1). Creation was seen primarily in the land which came into view as the primeval waters were parted and gathered into seas (Gen 1:6-10). The seas represented water which was technically outside of creation, extending down under the earth to the abyss which was outside of creation accessible to humanity. On earth the ruling crowns shift from the seven heads (12:3) to the ten horns which represent the fullness of human rulers, who lend their power to promoting human glory and, therefore, the evil of the beast. The seven heads show false titles to lead humanity to the evil goals, but without direct power. There is a vision in the book of Daniel of four animals that rise out of the sea (Dn 7:1-7), each representing an empire (Dn 7:17). The first beast was a lion representing the Babylonian empire, followed by a bear representing the Medes, than a leopard representing the Persians and, finally, a beast with iron teeth and bronze claws representing the Greek empire. Here the beast has likenesses to three of the four empires (13:2) but they are combined in a single beast. Therefore, these likenesses represent not the historical empires themselves as shown in Daniel, but the appearances of political power which can attempt to make itself the apparent center of creation in any age.

Historically, each nation had its own pagan gods to worship and a local ruler who functioned as the agent for the gods. Since pagan gods didn't actually exist as divine beings, the political power of the nation ruled on the basis of a pretense. Satan is known as the "father of lies" (Jn 8:44) and promoting the existence of pagan gods in the empires is surely the greatest of lies. There would be no reason for the people of a pagan nation to search for the True God under such circumstances since the belief was put forth that only the non-existent pagan gods could provide for the nation and protect it. Since there was no connection to a divine being, political power was in fact a substitute for a relationship with God even though that may not have been understood by anyone in the nation (3:9). To be separate from

God and offering worship to a non-existent divinity through a political system was evil in being in opposition to God.

The ability of an evil spirit to gain control in such a situation produced an image of the sea beast. This doesn't say that political power is evil, but focusing on itself and, in effect, worshiping itself without attempting to find God is by definition evil. It is a desire and a search for divinity separate from the only God. When the political power was an empire rather than a single nation, the effect was more pronounced as the empire attempted to extend its control to the whole world. It attempted to be the only example of ultimate power that could be seen on earth even though the totality of creation visible to humanity would always point to something greater than an empire which controlled only a part of the planet.

The pagan world judged divine power as something behind the political power that developed on earth. The effect of worldwide support for political power, that was so successful as to be in widespread control as an empire, is noted in the text (13:4). Individual nations with their own gods would appear as being somewhat equal with other nations. When only a single superpower exists, as is the case with a great empire, there would seem to be no power that could defeat it. Since the political power was projected as a sign of the divine power of the pagan gods, there would seem to be no competing divine power that could overcome those pagan gods. This was the condition that might have been seen as existing through most of the historical period of the world and, especially, outside of Judaism during the last centuries before Christ.

The blasphemies against God would occur automatically as the people offered worship and praise to the false gods (13:1). However, the terminology of those who supported the beast as being ones whose names were not "written down since the foundation of the world in the book of life of the sacrificial Lamb" (13:8) would seem to be something known from the vision rather than from a knowledge of Jesus Christ. This occurs at a time when the political power of Rome had become powerful in the Middle East and the vision was a warning that far from following such power, it would be the time for those who knew the True God to follow the covenant relationship most closely. However, those who failed to do so would be left without protection as seemed true in the time of Jeremiah and the exile. Christianity would make that change starting with the persecution of Nero and its understanding coming in the Gospel of Mark, which points to this vision being earlier than those events.

The second beast arising from the land may have had the appearance of one who served God but the exhortation and teaching that came from it was more like the dragon (13:11). The second beast from the land is from creation and has accepted the power and authority of the sea beast and served it. The second beast could be seen as the religious authorities in the empires which caused the nations to worship non-existent pagan gods. The second beast could produce signs which seemed sufficiently miraculous as to convince the people of the truth of such worship and the correctness of persecution against those who didn't worship the beast. The concept that words seem to come from a statue (13:15) is not explained but it would be hard for people to oppose such words even if they were only reported by pagan religious authorities and not actually heard by the people (e.g. Ex 20:18-21). Likewise, the control of a population with regulations (13:16-17) would be acceptable to everyone else if it was necessary to enforce a loyalty issue as a means of gaining continued protection from non-existent pagan gods.

The number of the beast (13:18) has often been seen as the number of the emperor Nero, as derived from his name written in Hebrew (NERON CAESAR but spelled NRWN QSR since vowels would not be included). This construction has not been entirely convincing since other names could be made to fit the number either in Hebrew or by shifting to other languages and numbering systems. At the time and place of the writing there could be a great number of people who might fit the designation. However, this number is not in the vision nor does it give information on dating of the vision even though it is often used that way. It would only show that this little explanation was used either when the vision material was written down, or most likely when translated, to explain the meaning of the beast. The shrewdness that is required would seem to center on using Hebrew or Aramaic as the language and source of numbers as much as on the choice of a name. However, it says nothing about the dating of the vision or the resulting identity of the author, but is only a later clarification as the writing is made known to others. The triple six would be the superlative of six as evil and, therefore, means most evil.

Perhaps a key factor in not equating the 666 with Nero is that such a choice would be most obvious to the Romans who best knew the Nero return story. If Nero was the present emperor or had recently died, he would be the first person considered. If the identity was to be hidden in a code, it makes no sense to choose the person most obvious to those from which the meaning should be hidden to prevent reprisals.

CHAPTER 14 - Judgment

The faithful from Israel appear with the Lamb on the Mountain of God at the site of the temple (Is 8:18) and they are prepared for judgment (14:1). They have the names of God and the Lamb on their heads. However, after the Gospel of John was written, Christianity came to know that a single name was applied to both. Therefore, this section must have come from an earlier time, and yet it points toward the conclusion of the Fourth Gospel that the name Yahweh used for God in the Old Testament also applied to Jesus. The faithful are singing the new song of the great change (5:9) as they are redeemed. The virginity statement (14:14) is in opposition to the charge of adultery, meaning idolatry, against "unfaithful Israel" in the Old Testament (Jer 2:20-32). Using the number twelve as part of 144,000 indicates they are Jewish and the perfection of Judaism. Prior to the coming of the Messiah it would be almost impossible for Gentiles to be free of idolatry or any "faults." However, if the writing were at the end of the first century, there would be Christian saints also. This great number from the twelve tribes have kept the name of the True God, never accepting subjugation of the two beasts. They are the "first fruits" which are dedicated to God (14:4) and in the covenant understanding the first fruits belonged to God. Therefore, to offer them meant they would be accepted by God. Truth is what comes from God in revelation and they have never stated anything but the truth (14:5).

This witness by the 144,000 made them ready for judgment and then an angel brings the announcement that judgment will begin (14:6-7). That Babylon has fallen is announced by a second angel (14:8). A third angel announces that those who have accepted the name of the beast, those who have not been constant in keeping the commandments of God and faith in Jesus, will see a judgment of punishment instead of glory and happiness (14:9-10). They have chosen to follow only a power on earth which very clearly could not have been the creator of earth and, therefore, was false and evil. They will get that choice and, if evil which misleads people will be punished, that punishment will be part of their choice. The ones who are subject to punishment are those loyal to the beast just as in the fifth trumpet (9:4). If this is an image of persecution in Revelation, the punishment is directed only at the opponents of the Lamb rather than his followers. It certainly doesn't fit with the understanding of persecution attributed to Domitian from the traditional context of this writing. The great affliction is the judgment and it is affliction only for those who haven't chosen life with God; those who chose God are saved (7:14-15).

The judgment is carried out by "one like a Son of Man" (Dn 7:13) coming from the power of heaven and first reaping in the grain from the earth. The yield of the first harvest will be taken to the cloud of the Son of Man or heaven (14:16). It consists of the life of the grain that is taken to a new site and a new life. The second harvest is of ripe grapes that are put through a wine press which produces a flood of blood. It spreads out for 200 miles as deep as a horse's bridle. The blood is life which is poured out on earth rather than returning to God; it has no seed to a new life in heaven. The Old Testament expectation of the Day of the Lord, being a time when wine would be so superabun-

dant that the mountains and hills would run with wine, comes to
be different than expected. The yield of the vintage stays on
earth as blood (life) poured out and wasted (14:19-20). There
were always warnings that the Day of the Lord would be filled
with gloom and terror for those who waited rather than prepared
and this description says the worst.

CHAPTER 15 - Seven Bowls

The next view of heaven includes those who had been
prepared and opposed the beast during life and are in heaven
having no part in troubles on earth (15:1-4). The serenity is
shown in the sea which is so completely under the control of
God that it is like glass and the presence of fire would indicate
the presence of God amid those who are saved. They sing the
new song of praise to God. The song is ascribed to both Moses
and the Lamb and certainly would reflect the praise of the Torah
considered to be the writing of Moses and the praise of this Book
which introduces the Lamb.

The seven bowls of plagues, which are intended to cause
people to look beyond earth for happiness, are said to be prepared from God's anger (15:7). However, the anger of God is
actually separation from God which the followers of the beast
have chosen. It is the rejection of the gift of union that God
offered to all the nations even though it was seen in the
covenant relationship starting with Israel and developed by
Judaism into a worldwide witness as they came to know the only
True God. The Jews lived throughout the world and yet rejected
any other religion while witnessing to God who was not part of
empires and the religious folly of the sea beast and land beast.
The problems and difficulties of nature should have made everyone look for a kingdom of promise. The evil that accompanied
the empires which relied on wars, punishments, and rigid con-
trols should have been a warning to look for something better.
The witness of Judaism pointed to a faith that went far beyond
empires and idol worship. Lastly, the signs of God offering a
union in heaven, as the plan of God was trumpeted and opened
to earth in the coming of a Messiah, should have been enough to

change the minds of everyone. Instead, the answer will be to resist God's coming all the more defiantly and curse the result for themselves as the bowls are emptied.

CHAPTER 16

The initial four bowls (16:1-9) are emptied on those on earth; the first on those who had chosen the beast and then the next three on the seas, on the rivers and springs and on the sun. Judaism understood since the time of the great Exodus event that God could control all of nature. Therefore, problems that come from nature must represent a lesson not to choose creation as the whole meaning of life. Pagans should recognize that Jews lived throughout the world, yet had no notion of their own protection nor would they see the empires as protection. They had existed while empires came and went and their religious loyalties were never to the gods of empires (Wis 2:1-3:12). The problems of nature must be God's constant warning to look beyond creation as the final meaning of God's gift.

The fifth bowl is emptied on the empire of the beast causing great pain, but those who are hurt curse God rather than choosing to change (16:10-11). Once in the grip of evil power, those who are pained become more dependent on that power and curse any witness to a better choice. The sixth bowl allows the enemies of God who come together in a union with evil to do battle with the Lamb (16:12-16). The warning about being "naked" refers to not having on the life of Christ and instead of going to the place of light (21:23), they would be cast into the darkness (Mt 22:13-14). The magnitude of God's greatness provides a certainty of failure for the enemies of God, but people can make their decision to rely on evil which is leading creation against the Creator who by definition must have power over creation. The seventh plague brings destruction on earth and those who are harmed curse God (16:17-21). Evil and those who worship it cannot accept that in choosing a life separate from God they have brought destruction to themselves. The last bowl brings the destruction of cities including the Great City which is called Babylon the Great, but is actually Jerusalem. This is the time of affliction when everyone must face judgment and would recognize they should have searched for the God of all creation and now seeing their failure would find the punishment most bitter.

CHAPTER 17 - The Harlot and Babylon

The interlude that was introduced prior to the seventh seal and seventh trumpet is introduced again after the seventh bowl to give a more detailed picture of what occurs before the judgment to the Great City and in the victory of the Lamb. The destruction of Jerusalem and the temple worship opens the sixth series of seven which brings the Messiah and ends in judgment and eternal reward for the faithful. All of this series are "the things that are still to come" at the time of the vision. They make the recording of the vision essential as they start becoming clear in the events of the first century.

The harlot is a common Old Testament image used to portray unfaithful Israel (Is 1:21). The clearest uses are by Hosea for the northern kingdom and by Ezekiel, in chapter 22 for Jerusalem, and in chapter 23 for Jerusalem and Samaria, or the whole of Israel. The earlier use of the term harlot in writing prior to the exile was as a judgment that in the keeping of the covenant relationship Israel had focused on a doing of sacrificial acts which were offered in the name of Yahweh, but which mimicked Canaanite sacrifices. In those earlier times such sacrifices were often offered on altars that were not at the temple and may have been jointly used by non-Israelites for their own sacrifices to pagan gods (2 Kgs 23:4-14). That was shown most clearly in descriptions of the northern kingdom Israel where there was no temple of Yahweh's but there were shrines and altars on high places often originating in Canaanite worship to pagan gods. However, the historical sections of 1 and 2 Kings indicate that the Israelites did not understand their practices to be a failure until the finding of the book of Deuteronomy in the temple in the time of Josiah (2 Kings 22:3-20). The reform of Josiah gives the details of what was changed after the Law was clarified. The exile to Babylon that followed only a short time after the reform raised the question of where Israel must have failed in keeping the covenant. The result was the gathering together of Israel's record of revelation in their history to produce an early version of the Old Testament in order to carry out a comprehensive reform to the problems.

After the Exile, the rebuilding of the temple (Ezr 3:1-4:5) and the public reading of that early Old Testament (Ne 8:1-3) would seem to be a determined effort to keep the Law as perfectly as possible. Yet at the same time Judaism came to the understanding that Yahweh is not just the God of Judaism, but is the only God for all creation. Even though shown in Second Isaiah (Is 44:9-20 most clearly), this change in perspective was revolutionary to the nth degree and wouldn't be accepted by other peoples of the world for a number of centuries. Judaism moved to a very different understanding of God than on what their own scriptural record was based. Furthermore, as the only people with this understanding, they could gain no assistance from the experiences of any other nation. They were called to live out a covenant relationship with God far different from what they originally knew or expected.

The period of the wisdom literature chronicles their groping and speculation on how their perspective of the covenant must change to be true to the whole revelation from the One God. That body of literature shows a questioning while at the same time there is an unwillingness to dramatically change the keeping of the Law probably for fear that another failure might bring a repetition of the Exile or worse. Jerusalem had the great message of God that must be meant for all people because there was only One God and, therefore, one Creator of all people. Yet, instead of inviting outsiders into the relationship, this was a time when Judaism became very separate from pagans. Where there is language about Jerusalem being responsible for the "blood of saints" (17:6) and "all the blood shed on earth" (18:24), it would apply to any people who failed to make the choice for a relationship with God because that option was not made obvious to them by Jerusalem. The vision is given to John to witness to the world at this time (10:11) and correct that failure of Jerusalem from the past which John the Baptist clearly understands (Mt 3:7-9).

The limited view available from that period of the previous millennium, the last four centuries prior to the coming of the Messiah, seems to be a keeping of the Law in a literal fashion with respect to temple sacrifices by the Sadducees as a response to what was the existing understanding. At the same time, at least after the revolt of the Maccabees, the Pharisees promoted a keeping of the Law in a more complete way through traditions of the elders which applied to all the people. Since the Law sections of the Pentateuch are directed overwhelmingly toward the temple operations, there was some disagreement between Sadducees and Pharisees about the relative importance of these two approaches. The Sadducees seemed to hold the position that the literal keeping of the temple rituals and sacrifices was the basis for the covenant and must be kept exactly and completely. They may have seen popular practices in keeping the Law in the personal lives of the Jewish people as clearly secondary and perhaps a digression that could lessen support for the temple functions. The Pharisees must have agreed with the temple operations being primary. However, following the speculative wisdom writings, they may have seen popular practices as a necessary development to carry the covenant response to a living of the Law by everyone rather than only a rigid and mechanical keeping of temple requirements. The repetition of "a line of Kings and Priests" in this Book as a double covenant relationship with God supports the Pharisee view, and goes beyond it when the temple is destroyed. The covenant is to be found in a lived relationship with God.

In such a view, the Sadducees would have a positive response toward a Roman presence that protected the nation and the temple from a war which would have resulted in a loss of the temple and, therefore, the means of keeping the Law. The Pharisees would recognize that possible value, but also would see the full living of the Law on a popular level as something that could be done most completely if all non-Jews were removed from the land given to them by Yahweh. As in most such differences in goals, what may have started with both groups being part of a holiness-oriented Hasidim community, changed through a hardening of their different approaches to covenant, and produced a significant division.

The Essenes, who seem most clearly as a remnant of the Hasidim, became anti-Sadducee through a difference in belief on how the temple was to be operated. Their argument with what the Sadducees were doing was sufficient to cause the Essenes to leave Jerusalem and, for at least some of them, to move to an isolated community in the desert at Qumran. Surely, the allowing of a Roman Procurator to be the one who selected the High Priest as his local agent must have been difficult to accept by the Essenes. A foreign pagan as the one who designates who should enter the Holy of Holies once each year and who would be the one who pronounced God's name a single time each year would have been unacceptable. Then also, the Romans had a practice of collecting all of the revenues derived from the payment of a Roman temple tax by Jews throughout the empire and giving those funds to the Jewish temple. Since such funds would have to be used as donations for sacrifices offered for the Roman empire, the whole connection of the temple to Rome must have seemed blasphemous to the Essenes.

It would appear that the temple under Sadducee operation was being used to support Rome and essentially maintain Roman control in a land given by God to Judaism. Pharisee opposition may have resulted in the formation of a Zealot group among the Pharisees to provoke an uprising against Rome and start the process of removing all Gentiles from the land. However, the abandonment by the Essenes of a presence in Jerusalem and at the temple was the far greater witness. John the Baptist's strong condemning language against a group of Pharisees and Sadducees (Mt 3:6-8) when they come to him at the Jordan River certainly expresses the Essene view and seems to make John one of that sect. However, his condemnation of temple operations would surely come from the destruction of Jerusalem shown in the vision even if John the Baptist was not an Essene.

This is the background for interpretation of chapter 17

where the condemnation of the religious leaders of the temple under the title of harlot and under the name Babylon should be seen. The people called out of the Great City when it is destroyed and away from the temple practices would be Judaism in general (18:4-8). That calling out could have occurred prior to the city's destruction as it actually happened in the first century in which case the leaving in 66 for Pella by the Christian side of Judaism could have been a result of this warning. However, the warning from John the Baptist would have been for all of Judaism (Mt 3:9).

The harlot in chapter 17 is Jerusalem in a special way as the place where God "chose to give His name a home" or have it enthroned in the temple. She is a response to the covenant which makes the temple operation dependent on the Roman empire for protection and that is the witness given to all the people of the world (17:15) or as stated, "who rules enthroned beside abundant waters" (17:1). Judaism had spread out to many nations, perhaps 80% of the Jews lived outside of Palestine, so the opportunity to witness to the covenant existed throughout the world. Yet, when only Jews were welcomed to Jerusalem for the feasts and Jews elsewhere were directed to be separate from Gentiles, the responsibility for worldwide witnessing to the whole truth did not occur. The harlot's interest would be in a sterile repetition of rituals which are seen as most important in keeping the covenant through a literal keeping of the Law. That is the very failure condemned by the prophets against pre-exilic Israel (Is 1:11-17, Am 5:21-24). The harlot offers the animal sacrifices in the temple to the name but not to the true meaning of One God for all of creation. Rather, the offering is to a narrow and bland reading of the words of the Law. It was the method of sacrifice that would be used for a pagan god in other countries. The witness of the Messiah was to interrupt the means of such sacrifices on his first journey to Jerusalem (Jn 2:13-25). This witness was enhanced and clarified in Jesus' statement about how worship must change (very soon) that was made to the woman at the well (Jn 4:21-24).

The harlot is accused of fornication with all the kings of

the earth because her method of offering sacrifice was in doing an action of killing animals rather than bringing about a living relationship with God. That was the same as what the pagans did in their temples under the rule of kings who acted as agents of pagan gods. The temple that bears God's name should have been a worldwide witness to God and the covenant, but all that the population of the world would actually see from the harlot would be a resemblance of what occurred in pagan temples. Regardless of what the temple leaders attempted to portray as the meaning of keeping the Law, the actual witness would be seen very differently by the world.

The identification of the harlot as Jerusalem and its destruction must be examined carefully to gain the full understanding that is presented in Revelation. The destruction of Jerusalem is a judgment against some aspect of Jewish life and, since the temple was destroyed, the suspicion would be that the judgment is against how temple worship was carried out. Judaism would come to that conclusion, even without the Book of Revelation, when the temple is destroyed in 70 near the end of the Jewish revolt. However, in the view of John the Baptist, the destruction would not be a judgment against Judaism as a whole since more than 80% of the Jews live outside of Palestine and were directly affected by the destruction of the temple only in terms of an occasional pilgrimage to Jerusalem for a feast. The judgment also would not be against the Jewish people living specifically in Jerusalem or Palestine since the response of a "new voice" from heaven is to call the people away from the destruction and whatever caused it to happen (18:4). The people living under such temple activity are called to salvation through a means which does not include having a temple worship.

A case might be made for condemning those operating the temple, such as the priests that serve in the temple or the Sadducees who promote a literal keeping of the Law with animal sacrifices. Yet, even those groups would not be condemned if they left behind such sacrifices as worship when called out of "Babylon," and indeed, they must have done just that when the temple was destroyed. The condemnation is of an interpretation of how the covenant relationship was lived after the concept of God had changed so dramatically in the previous few centuries with Judaism coming to know there was only One True God for all of creation.

The basis for animal sacrifices must have had its starting point in a sacrificial system shared with the early Canaanites. Surely, animal sacrifices to pagan gods was the standard practice among pagans in all the countries surrounding Palestine. When it was obvious to Judaism that the view of Yahweh was dramatically different from the pagan view of their gods, why would the sacrificial system remain the same?

Early prophets had criticized the response of the Israelites to the covenant relationship. The charges of adultery against Israel carries the meaning of worshiping other gods rather than Yahweh. Yet, in the account of Josiah's reform (2 Kgs 22:3-23:27) there is no indication that Israel was worshiping other gods. Rather, the worship of Yahweh seemed to occur, at least in part, at altars or sites that may have accommodated sacrifices by Canaanites and other non-Israelites to pagan gods. Josiah makes a point of desecrating completely the northern Israel shrine at Bethel which must have had its primary use by Israelites. However, if a shrine was not the place chosen by Yahweh for a presence on earth, such sacrifices by Israelites were condemned, even though their intention was to honor God. The early condemnation of the kings of the northern kingdom carried a standard note that a king had "copied the example of Jeroboam son of Nabat and the sins into which he had led Israel" (1 Kgs 16:26) by offering sacrifices at shrines away from the temple.

Therefore, it is important to note that the condemnation that occurs in the destruction of the harlot is directed at the way the temple was operated rather than Judaism or the Jewish people. Seeing this criticism directed at such practices prior to the coming of the Messiah gives a very different view of God's intent than having it occur after the time of Jesus. Here God is sending a prophet to change the understanding and the Messiah will offer salvation to the world, but starting in Judaism. Certainly the first of "the called, the chosen, the faithful" (17:14) are the

Jewish people who respond to God's offer. Judaism is the focus of the last and greatest element of the entire revelation from God, because they are the only people who could understand it. Jews coming from synagogues throughout the world to Jerusalem for the pilgrimage feasts and returning were the initial element in causing an awareness of the Messiah to be known among Jews throughout the world. From the overseas synagogues the message would go beyond Judaism, first to Godfearers who attended the synagogues, and then to Gentiles accepted into Christian communities which had become separated from the synagogues. When this Book is read as the initial introduction of the Messiah, Jesus' words will qualify the way John has presented the vision from Old Testament quotations just as the Old Testament view of the Messiah was changed by the Gospel writings.

In the desert, the harlot is riding a scarlet beast with seven heads and ten horns (17:3) which is the description of the evil dragon of chapter 12 rather than the sea beast of chapter 13. To offer animal sacrifices to false gods or to offer the same type of sacrifices to the True God is the deception put forth by the dragon to deceive all the world. The dragon makes war on "all who obey God's commandments" (12:17) and, in hiding the meaning of the covenant behind practices of constant animal sacrifices, the dragon intends to win that war.

The harlot wears garments of purple and scarlet (17:4), the colors specifically required for the vestments of the temple priests starting with Aaron (Ex 28:1-7, 15). The same colors may represent royal political power as the garments of emperors and the reflection of the scarlet beast always attempting to be seen through corrupt political and religious powers. However, here John's interpretation of the harlot is of a sacrificial system that seems to not recognize that the Jewish view of God and covenant had changed in the last few centuries, while the sacrificial system remained with an old view. Therefore, the vestment garments would reflect the static view of sacrificial worship from the Law which becomes false worship when the knowledge of God is changed. The sacrificial system is condemned rather than the destruction being a condemnation of Judaism or the people of Jerusalem.

The harlot is satisfied to remain enthroned in the desert, to look only for a kingdom on earth rather than the true kingdom of God. She carries a golden wine cup as a symbol of the importance of temple utensils, yet if what is in the cup is not the offering God has requested from religious leaders, surely it would be filled with the evil offerings for a pagan sacrifice (Ez 23:33-34). The temple sacrifices are seen as continuing to fulfill the Law even though the prophets called upon the people to change and be loving, just as God is loving and just (Am 5:21-24).

The name Babylon has been written on her head (17:5) instead of the name of God which should have been enthroned in the temple practices. The writer does not indicate this could be interpreted by shrewdness, but rather that it is a mystery. There is no direct connection between Jerusalem and Babylon in the Old Testament. However, there is a very strong condemnation of Babylon in chapter 51 of Jeremiah which is alluded to in this section of Revelation and in the calling away of the people from this city (18:1-8). The original Babylon had been called an agent of Yahweh in the Exile, but Babylon was too cruel to the Israelites so that the plan of Yahweh was not carried out and, therefore, Babylon was destroyed (Jer 25:8-13). Surely it would be a mystery for Judaism, the only nation to know the True God, to remain with animal sacrifices and put trust in a pagan empire to protect a temple building and city so that the covenant would not be broken by a failure to follow the sacrificial prescription of the Law.

The mystery of the name must be figured out in order to understand the correlation between the temple practices which fail to show the true covenant and Babylon as an earlier agent of God who likewise failed and was destroyed. So the condemnation of Babylon by the prophet becomes the description of what would have to occur to Jerusalem as well. She should have become more concerned with those outsiders who would have become holy and searched for a closeness in life with the One God in the covenant had the covenant invitation been extend-

ed to them. However, the closeness accepted by those who provided religious leadership at the temple was with an empire that
seemed to provide protection but had a connection with the
beast. If John had an Essene background, this would resonate
with their experience even before Christianity would arise with
the death of Christ in a plot between Jewish leaders, afraid to
face a threat to the temple, and a Roman procurator, afraid of
any demonstrations to a ruler not subject to pagan gods.

The explanation of the beast by the angel (17:8-11) is
often turned into a discussion of Roman emperors by commentators even though the text doesn't support such an excursion.
Likewise, if the Book is read as the revelation of the coming of
Jesus as the Messiah, the whole discussion of emperor names
vanishes in meaning just as any attempt to name the ten kings is
left out. There had not been enough emperors of Rome to satis-
fy the description that early in the first century. Then the discussion of the seven heads must shift to what is known from the
Old Testament about empires as is everything else in the Book.

The sea beast description (13:1-10) points toward evil
political power over a long time span and reflects the beasts of
the book of Daniel. In Daniel 7, there are four manifestations of
beasts rising from the sea which represent the empires of
Babylon, the Medes, Persia, and the Greeks. The sea beast of
Revelation 13 clearly has characteristics of the first three of
those empires and that beast exercises the evil power of the red
dragon of Revelation 12. While the ruling power of the dragon
in heaven was described as coronets being on the heads, when
the power is transferred to the sea beast the coronets are transferred to the horns, which represent human rulers who carry out
the interests of the beast.

The angel describes the beast John has seen as one who
once was and now is not, but who will come up from the abyss to
be destroyed in the future (17:8). What John has seen earlier is
the dragon who was thrown down to earth (12:9) and into the
abyss (9:1) and later as a separate entity with the beast and false
prophet. Satan will mobilize nations in the war against God
which is part of the sixth bowl (16:13). That would be the

return of the dragon who is overpowered and chained for a thousand years (20:2-3) only to be freed and allowed to deceive all the nations of the world (20:8) and go to his destruction. The angel's explanation seems to come quite clearly from the vision given to John without a long discussion about Roman emperors and a great amount of speculation on information that only would be known from non-biblical sources at the end of the first century. If the people who are deceived by the dragon are those who "marveled" at the beast (13:3) or thought his return "miraculous" (17:8), it's because they only see the beast as the political power of an empire which represents the dragon on earth. The angel knows the dragon as the source of evil and John has been introduced to the dragon in the vision but the world only sees the manifestation of such power in the empires (the coming and going of the power of the beast).

The "need for cleverness" interlude (17:9), as with an earlier interlude (13:18), is not part of the angel's explanation, but comes from a later writer to make clear how the representation can be understood at the time of the writing or its translation into Greek for another audience. The identification of the evil beast with the Roman empire at the time of the writing would be in equating the seven hills with the seven heads. The harlot "sitting on them" is Jerusalem supported by the Roman empire rather than the city of Rome built on seven hills which would only serve as a geological base for the city rather than a live beast as the angel's description indicates. Later, the beast will attack the harlot (17:16) which is meaningless if it means the geological base of seven hills is going to attack the city of Rome built on those hills. However, the Roman empire attacking Jerusalem that Rome had supported and to which Rome gave at least local and religious control is both logical and, of course, actually happened during the time of the Jewish revolt in Palestine.

The seven heads representing seven emperors (17:10) is a return to the angel's classification and wouldn't mean seven Roman emperors because the seven heads are the beast in all of its historical manifestations as empires. The emperors would represent empires throughout history, most directly those who started empires, and, therefore, means the complete use of political power to gain control of the earth. The five that are past would include at least the four empires of Daniel 7. However, Judaism certainly would include the Assyrians as one of the evil empires since they took away the entire northern kingdom which represented about three-quarters of the Israelites. The Assyrians are not included in Daniel since the setting of that book seems to start with the Babylonians after the Assyrian empire disappeared.

The Roman empire would be the sixth as it is the present empire at the time of the vision and writing. The seventh empire would only have meaning of completeness of empires and, therefore, isn't identified but would be the manifestation of evil rulers in the world who would attempt to overcome God's people (12:17) rather than a listing of all possible rulers or some artificial choosing of names. The return of the dragon would be the eighth and also of the seven (17:11) since the promotion of non-existence pagan gods or false worship to the True God is always part of Satan's plan. Revelation is a message of God's plan, not a search for names to fill in the blanks on a list of names. Only in trying to make this a late writing, by substituting conditions and information from non-biblical sources, would anyone attempt to give names of emperors to the "five gone," the one present, the one yet to come and the "eighth."

The ten horns as ten kings (17:2) still to receive power is the fullness of pagan rulers who will fight the King of Kings rather than individual rulers that can be named. In this case, commentators rarely make an attempt to give names to the kings. A reference could be made to the ten kings of Daniel 7:24 but they were the fullness of kings at that time. The fullness of kings at a later time will be those who fight for the beast at that later time. They are included as a statement that no combination of kings and rulers can ever overcome the King of Kings by using the power of evil. Particular note should be made of how the victory over the ten kings is achieved. It is by the followers of the King of Kings, "the called, the chosen and the faithful" (17:14). This is a victory that results from the King of Kings coming from heaven into creation and also being present in a body that has accepted the commandments as gift from God. The temple is destroyed after the Resurrection because in the death and Resurrection the true sacrifice acceptable to God is known and offered continuously in the Eucharist. There is no need for animal sacrifices any more and God's name is removed from a place for such sacrifices and given to the people who will take part continuously in the true sacrifice.

The changed description of the harlot from being "enthroned beside abundant waters" (17:1), as was the original Babylon with its agricultural development, to "all the peoples, populations, nations, and languages" (17:15) also fits Jerusalem. Jewish people lived in all major cities and were always identifiable by their keeping of the Sabbath and their separate kosher foods. The areas where these cities were located was far greater than the area of the Roman empire since it included the great areas to the east of Palestine, as well as the Arabian peninsula and Ethiopia, in addition to the cities of the Roman empire. The ability of Judaism to witness was great and had they emphasized inviting pagans to become Jewish, it is reasonable to assume the effort would have been successful. However, their fear of associating with Gentiles after suffering the Exile in Babylon, which they thought was due to an association with pagan sacrifice sites (2 Kgs 23:26-27), seemed to prevent such invitations. However, that part of Judaism that accepted the Messiah produced the early evangelization starting with that synagogue connection.

The battle that is most distinct is the turning of the ten kings and the beast, a political action, against the harlot (17:16). The quotation of "strip off her clothes and leave her naked" could be taken as destroying the city walls, but as a quotation from Ezekiel 16:37, it is the destruction of unfaithful Jerusalem to make clear who is being destroyed. However, since the protection which Jerusalem always relied upon was the presence of Yahweh in the temple, this meaning would relate to the destruction of the temple as well. The eating of flesh could mean killing the inhabitants or deporting them, and burning the remains means that there is no remnant of the temple remaining to rebuild in the future. The destruction seems to be a reference to Jeremiah 51:58 giving the final statement on ancient Babylon. However, the description is about the same as for the destruction of Jerusalem by Babylon (Jer 52:12-14).

Those who destroyed the harlot are called agents of God in the same way as the Babylonians were agents during the Exile (17:17). In reality, once God had withdrawn protection from the city, any political force that destroyed it would be carrying out the work of God in showing clearly that it was not God's will that the city should be protected and saved. The final note (17:18) that the "harlot is the great city that had authority over all the rulers on earth" not only ties Babylon and the Great City together but also defines it as Jerusalem. Authority over other rulers would come because God ruled in the temple of Jerusalem. Rome would not have authority over other cities; it would have only military and political force to gain control. Rome would not be considered for Babylon if the end of the first century context were not used for the visions. It could well be that the availability of this Book in Greek was an important element in early Christianity's acceptance of the temple destruction and the reason why such an event did not enter other New Testament writings.

CHAPTER 18

This chapter opens with a repeat of the earlier declaration of an angel about Babylon's fate (14:8) and part of the charges made against her as the harlot (17:2,5), tying the three sections together as different views of the same event. Then follows a condemnation of Babylon which has no real meaning if it was a city or nation that never knew God in the first place. The statement that "her sins have reached up to heaven" (18:5) indicates that Babylon must have known the meaning of sin. If sin is seen as separation from God, the meaning that arises from Jewish Law, every nation is completely separated from God if they have no knowledge of God. Only Jerusalem which has been graced by the presence and knowledge of the True God could have sinned in a way which was particularly offensive. Paul wrote to the Romans that he didn't know "what sin was except for the Law" and "when there is no Law, sin is dead" (Rom 7:7-11). If Babylon is condemned severely for sin, Babylon must know the Law as a covenant relationship and be expected to abide by it. That would fit Jerusalem perfectly, but could not be said of Rome or any other pagan city.

The description of Jerusalem comes from the description of the punishment of ancient Babylon by Jeremiah in 51:5-6. "Escape (or flee) out of Babylon, do not perish yourselves in her punishment" reflects 18:4. "Babylon was a golden cup in Yahweh's hand, she made the whole world drunk (from her wine), the nations drank her wine and went mad" (Jer. 51:7) refers to 17:4 and 18:3. Likewise, Jeremiah 51:36-37 telling of "rivers and springs running dry, the city a heap of stones seeming as a lair of jackals, a thing of horror with no one living in it" certainly reflects "the haunt of devils" (18:2). The quotes of being a "queen on my throne" saying "I am no widow" (18:7) comes from Isaiah 47:7-9 with the result occurring in a "single day" (18:8). What had been said by the prophets about ancient Babylon is transferred here to Jerusalem. That transfer of meaning as temple worship shifts from what is necessary to keep the covenant to actions which are condemned solves the mystery of the name (17:5). The agent of God who doesn't follow the plan of God ceases to be an agent, first as seen in Babylon in the Exile by the Israelites who recognized God's involvement when the temple was destroyed, and here again if this temple comes to the same result.

The "single hour" (18:10) like the "single day" (18:8) could stand for a lifetime of an ordinary person or the importance of a lifetime. In giving this as a warning, which was proclaimed to everyone, it would indicate that many of them would see the destruction and, therefore, should act on this warning. The destruction of the temple would occur about 45 years later in 70. At that event everyone connected to Judaism (as Christians were) would wonder if they were condemned by God (or abandoned by God). However, if this vision were known at the time of the temple destruction, it would be clear that such destruction was part of the plan of God which was fulfilled, as the entire plan would be fulfilled. In the crucifixion and resurrection, everyone who heeded the prophesy would see that Christ had conquered all that evil could bring as a punishment on this earth which would be human death. With the sharing of life with God in Christ, there is no loss for anyone living that sharing of life. They had in baptism given up life in this world to put on and start living the eternal life (Rom 6:4). Therefore, the disciples of the Lamb could not be harmed by anything brought by evil and, therefore, evil is defeated by the coming of the Messiah (17:14).

The mourning and weeping by kings, traders, and seafarers (18:9-19) who were associated with Jerusalem causes difficulties in understanding because history doesn't record these relationships. Yet, Jerusalem had a special duty to witness to the entire world about the meaning of a covenant with God and its availability to everyone. What actually was shown by Jerusalem included a relationship with the Roman empire in which Jerusalem accepted Roman protection. Jerusalem did not seem so different from the other kingdoms which accepted Roman protection to obtain "peace" rather than relying on God. Jerusalem offered the same type of sacrifices as pagan temples and some sacrifices were for God's protection of the Roman empire. The "mourning and weeping" occur because what had happened to one kingdom within the empire could visit the other kingdoms as well.

To the traders of the world who promoted commerce with Jerusalem by sending cargos of goods of this world and exporting similar goods, everything seemed the same as all other countries (18:15-16). Jerusalem had the same need for linen and dyes and expensive decorations as the other kingdoms and seemed no different from other customers. Yet, Jerusalem had one commodity for export which the whole world required, a relationship with God, and it was never exported. Even in pagan countries where the synagogues were open to non-Jews who came and accepted Jewish beliefs, there was no attempt to bring them into the full relationship until Christian times when these "Godfearers" could accept the Christian relationship and bypass many of the Jewish requirements of the Law.

The seafarers (18:17-19) might present a slightly different situation in that Jews from all parts of the world came as pilgrims to the temple at the time of the three major feasts of Passover, Pentecost and Tabernacles. Many of these people would travel by sea and must have produced extra revenue for ships hauling goods which made the journeys necessary in the first place. Passengers would load themselves, feed themselves, and find places to sleep on board. Passengers would be charged a fee for travel but there would be no extra cost to the ship. Destruction of the temple would immediately result in a great measurable loss of income for the seafarers. No other people traveled in such numbers from all parts of the empire to worship at a single temple. However, the other side of carrying these passengers would be that the passengers could have witnessed to the value of their relationship with God through the temple and the necessity of these journeys. Yet the journeys were never to result in an invitation to the crews traveling the same routes to take part in the feasts or even to explain their meaning. The means of bringing God's revelation to the world existed, but it was not intended to produce fruit.

So the action of the angel to show how Babylon would not be seen again (18:20-24) is no different from what occurred with the temple in operation—it was not seen. For religious leaders to hide a revelation meant for the world from nearly all the people of the world was condemned in the Old Testament (Ez 33:7-9) and should be seen as the deeper meaning behind some of Jesus' parables about the kingdom (Mt 21:33-46). Those called to celebrate are the saints, apostles and prophets (18:20). They would have been the ones, both Jews and Christians, who criticized the way the temple and the covenant relationship was presented to the world and lived out. They would celebrate because that which they had lived, and in some cases died for, would at last become a blessing for everyone as it had been for them. The songs and music, the craftsmanship, and voices of those celebrating were beautiful and memorable, but were never a praise of God open to the world. The failure was a repeat of what had been concluded from the Exile (Ba 2:22-23).

However, the dedication of lives (18:24), even the shedding of blood and the giving up of their lives in witnessing to the fullness of the revelation, was the great witness to the world that should have existed. Since blood means life in Judaism, the phrase "All the blood that was ever shed on earth" could refer to the life wasted by those who might have made a different choice if they had known about God's gift (2 Kgs 21:16). The gift of eternal life was meant for everyone but the failure to witness to them resulted in some not accepting the gift. That is the true loss because God intended everyone to have eternal life. The loss of life for a holy one is only life in the world; the loss of eternal life is the true tragedy.

CHAPTER 19 - Victory

The completion of emptying the bowls of the plan of God on the earth (16:17-21) results in a great celebration in heaven (19:1-10). "The noise of a huge crowd (Dan 10:6), like the sound of the ocean (Ez 43:2) or the great roar of thunder (10:4) answering" (19:6) is the proclamation of Jesus' public life starting to be heard as he prepared to take the new Jerusalem as a bride. The great multitudes including the 144,000 sealed (7:9) that had received their white robes and were waiting for their reward in heaven would be praising God. Heaven would be open to those of every nation, race, tribe, and language as intended in the plan of God from its opening. They represent the community of God who will become the bride of Christ, those who become one in life with Christ. The angel calls them blessed (19:9).

At this point John kneels before the angel to worship him and is told to stop since the angel is only a servant also. This scene is repeated at the end of the Book (22:9) and points to the early date of the vision for such a misunderstanding to occur. Judaism had a tradition that the Law was delivered to earth by angels. The earliest versions of the giving of the Law on Mt. Sinai tells of God's presence there speaking directly to Moses. Later, in the northern kingdom of Israel, such direct contact with God was not used and an angel was seen as an intermediary.

After the Exile, when Judaism came to understand that there is only One God for all of creation, their reverence toward God resulted in them not using the Divine Name. The substitution of angels as intermediaries became a means of not stating that there had been direct conversations with God in obtaining revelation. It would seem then that the angels as heavenly beings received more reverence also and this kneeling would be an example of that. The closeness of a sharing of life with God automatically would be a difficult concept to accept within Judaism and wouldn't be easily understood by John the Baptist. This reverence to the angel might be a recognition of a message from God and the reverence could be toward the message. The result of this message is that John will be the proclaimer of this vision, and so occupy the same position as witness. So there may be no special reverence for the angelic witness. However, in the vision, John is seeing and speaking with a being connected to heaven and the normal description of such a being would be a messenger or an angel. There would not have been any other non-divine beings in heaven other than angels.

In the text there is a mixing of titles between meanings that relate to God which are also related to the Lamb and to angels. John's reverence may reflect his own awe at what is being made known to him and how it is shown. He wouldn't know how to act or what to say and the kneeling would occur just from the normal reverence of Judaism (Mk 9:6). However, in a later first century context, there would be either a recognition of the identity of the "angel" or no kneeling would occur.

A battle between the King of Kings and earthly rulers in the last half of the chapter ends in a defeat of the forces of evil. The white horse and its rider, which disappeared immediately in the very opening of the plan of God after the breaking of the first seal (6:2), returns to the vision. The rider, "called faithful

and true," and "known by the name, The Word of God," is clearly Christ. "King of Kings" and "Lord of Lords" would fit the
long-awaited Messiah for Jews prior to his first coming. The
white horse and rider of the first seal (6:2), as the starting point
of the plan of God, included a rainbow or covenant but the
intervention of evil meant that the covenant bearer didn't stay
with humanity (12:5). That rider was "to rule all of the nations
with an iron scepter." Now the rider has a "name written on
him known only to himself" which would be "Yahweh." There
would be no reason to say "known only to himself" after the
Gospel of John makes it known to all Christianity and it could
be speculated that the community of John the Evangelist might
look for clues to the name in Jesus' sayings after reading this part
of Revelation.

If the white horse rider represents both the rider of the
horse of the first seal (6:2) and the child taken up by God (12:5),
then it is easy to see that the scroll with seven seals is the whole
plan of God as proposed earlier. After God came to earth in the
Incarnation and taught in the public life of Jesus, it would not be
necessary at the end of the first century for a vision to be given
that tells of the plan of God and to prepare for a return because
of a Roman persecution. Mark's Gospel was written to respond
to questions arising from Nero's persecution and the second
coming was specifically addressed in chapter 13 of that Gospel.
The sequence of the same scene given three different times and
each for a different purpose also indicates the structure of the
Book of Revelation. It proposes a meaning (plan of God) and
then clarifies the meaning using Old Testament texts (12:1-17)
and also prepares for the coming of the Messiah (19:11-21)
which is the event at hand at the time of the vision and the
Book's purpose.

"His cloak was soaked in blood" (19:13) indicates, in our
view, that the crucifixion has occurred prior to the defeat of the
beast and the chaining of the dragon. The defeat of evil occurs
in the Resurrection. The death of a person convicted of a capi-
tal offense by hanging on a tree meant the one so hanged was
cursed by God (Dt 21:22-23) but Christ, raised from the dead,

was clearly blessed and, therefore, is above the Law and that blessing is available to all who accept the life of Christ. It is that promise shown so clearly in the Resurrection that defeats evil, since anyone knowing of the gift from God would never choose allegiance to evil. The multitudes who accept the gift have their own lives (robes) made white in the blood of the Lamb through the acceptance of that blood (life of Christ) and become part of the bride of the Lamb (19:8), later called the Holy City or the new Jerusalem (21:2). They take part in the defeat of evil, as shown by riding on white horses also as the armies of heaven (19:14), since they have seen the power of evil and even felt its effects, and yet have chosen union with God. That witness defeats evil because evil cannot reign where no one chooses to be controlled by evil.

The forces of evil will die just as described by Ezekiel about the destruction of Gog (Ez 39:17-20) with their flesh being eaten by birds. For those who die in union with the Lamb, there is everlasting life. For those who die in union with evil, there is just so much dead flesh with no value except as carrion. The phrase "a sword to strike the pagans with" (19:15) hardly seems like a late writing when the church was open to Gentiles, but would be common as a thought earlier if written during a Jewish time. The sword that comes from his mouth is the gospel message that defeats evil by showing the love of God in revealing the gift of eternal life. The beast and false prophet are thrown into everlasting punishment and become a casualty of the defeat. False political power and false religious direction may exist in the world, but cannot gain complete control again because of the followers of the King of Kings witnessing in the world. Where Christianity becomes known, the pagan religions associated with empires, or relying on animal sacrifices, tend to disappear.

This battle and victory of the "King of Kings" (19:11-21) is another version of what was mentioned in the destruction of the harlot (17:14) to show that the victory comes in the Resurrection. The cloak soaked in blood (19:13) indicates Jesus' death and Resurrection brings the victory (Jn 12:31). It is the establishment of a kingdom on earth where God reigns in the hearts and bodies of whoever puts on the life of Christ and is called church, perhaps described most clearly in Matthew's confession of Peter (Mt 16:16-20). Naturally, for Christian communities that don't see the establishment of church as a continuation of Jesus' rule in the kingdom, and, perhaps, believe church communities to be only human organizations in opposition to St. Paul's expression of the body of Christ (1 Cor 12:12-30), the duration of the battle would be unclear. However, the battle has nothing to do with killing people on earth, no matter how evil they may seem to be, but of offering eternal life to any who will put on that life and live it on earth. To not be a disciple who brings the offer of God's gift to others would mean that person was not on the side of Christ in the battle.

In the living of the life of the Body of Christ, the witness of the gift is given to the world. Everyone is invited and that life of Christ becomes the actual life of a person when the world ends for that person or in its entirety. The battle is won by the gospel message of Christ, but the battle also is won in his followers, "the called, the chosen, the faithful" (17:14), who make up the "army" of the rider (19:19). How else are the multitudes to be sealed, either from Judaism with its long faithfulness to Yahweh (7:5-8) or the "people from every nation, race, tribe and language" who are "impossible to count"? This revelation indicates they will make their decision through a witness that is before them everyday and that same understanding is echoed in Jesus' words in the gospel (Lk 12:1-59). The use of the bride and bridegroom language (19:7-9) is so intensely descriptive because in a wedding each partner states an "I DO" to a single life together.

The old Jerusalem was a place where a covenant was attempted through the offering of the lives of animals to God. Judaism emphasized exactness in keeping the Law in the temple worship even as they came to know there was only One God for all creation. With a change in knowing God they should have changed their view of animal sacrifices. The new Jerusalem is where humanity has accepted the life of God for eternity in response to the Messiah heralded in this Book of Revelation.

Those who fail, or in the description of a battle are defeated, are those who chose only life on earth and they, too, were given what was chosen.

CHAPTER 20 - Final Judgment

The dragon in being chained has no direct power on earth, but still has influence because of those who choose the world rather than life with God. However, after the defeat of the beast and the dragon by the King of Kings, the presence of God reigns in the world due to the victory of Christ and the spread of his church (Jn 16:33).

Those who have witnessed for Jesus and have made that witness the testimony of their lives shall also reign with him even before the judgment (20:4 and Jn 3:36). Their lives have imitated Jesus so completely that they have shared his life on earth and it shall be theirs in heaven without waiting for the final judgment (Jn 5:24). They have become part of the first Resurrection, including those under the altar in the fifth seal who are accepted as a sacrifice with the Lamb and enter heaven immediately when it is opened by the victory of Jesus. They are never sent to Sheol. While the language of John relates this reward to those "beheaded for having witnessed for Jesus" (20:14), anyone who exchanges a life without Jesus for a life reflecting Jesus' life in baptism and then lives that life (Rom 6:5-11) would have accomplished the same end and gained the same reward.

The 1,000-year reign is one of an undetermined long period when the seal of God is placed on the foreheads of those who chose a sharing of life with God. The actual length of the reigning period is based on how long it will take for the Good News to be proclaimed to all of the nations (Mk 13:9-10). When the period comes to the end the dragon will be released to deceive all the nations (20:7-8). Since the beast is not present at this time, the devil will not be seen as an empire but may be seen as some type of worldwide movement which peoples and nations can choose to follow. Those who have chosen to have only what is in the world will fight against the disciples of Jesus in an attempt to deceive them with the false message of the dragon but they will be defeated. The fire that "will come down on them from heaven" (Ez 38:22) becomes, in this vision, the presence of God entering creation in the judgment (11:19).

Actually there will be no battle because their defeat will occur by their having chosen the world and the dragon rather than God as the Day of Judgment comes upon them. If the witness of the disciples had been clear and certain, there would have been less reason for anyone to choose the dragon rather than God. It is so certain that God will win because creation will pass away and those who chose only the life of the world will have chosen nothingness or a punishment of no love and no happiness for eternity.

The disappearance of creation brings judgment, but it is not clear to whom the judgment will extend. Those whose lives are filled with Jesus or end in a witness for Jesus will have given up any other life than one which imitates Jesus' own life. If that is the only life they have at the end, there would be no fear of final judgment since there is no second death (20:6) for them. Those who clearly chose the world at the end have received that nothingness or whatever misery comes with it.

In between are those who had some awareness of Jesus or had heard the Good News itself and have given some evidence of attempting to live the life of Christ but also living, at least partly, the life of the world. Their lives will be examined in the books "which were a record of what they had done in their lives" and on that they will be judged (Mt 25:31-46). There seems to be no suggestion of salvation coming from only a simple religious affiliation but only from how they lived the Lord's own life. If those of the first resurrection are an indication of all judgment, it will be on how they witnessed for Jesus (Mt 10:32-33). Death and Hades also are thrown into the burning lake with all those whose names could not be found written in the book of life. The burning lake would seem to be an everlasting punishment for evil (20:10) and those who choose the world. However, even the realization of how foolish it would be for anyone to choose some temporary advantage in the world, in face of the promise by the Creator of the world of an eternal life in happiness, would be a "most terrible" punishment (16:21).

CHAPTER 21 - Heavenly Jerusalem

The heavenly Jerusalem arrives as a complete replacement of the existing creation. Judaism had waited for a kingdom on earth with the temple where God chose to give his name a home. The plan of God has humanity, that has accepted God's offer of life, living in a heavenly kingdom with God. Jews had been unwilling in the previous few centuries to even say God's name, yet the reality of the gift turns out to be a life with God given to all who choose that option and live it. It isn't a case of Judaism failing to understand, so much as a case that God always gives so much more than anyone could ever expect or imagine. The "bride" is the union of humanity and divinity in the body of Christ or the Church. There will be no fear of a second death for those who prove victorious. "To those who prove victorious" (21:6-7) was repeated in each of the seven letters and it is the promise of the Lord throughout the plan of God. To prove "victorious" may have appeared difficult and uncertain in the seven letters but it becomes the opposite as the message of Christ is given in His public life and lived out in the present age.

The new Jerusalem appears as a glorious cube made of precious stones and metals. The gates through the walls, three on each side, are named after the twelve tribes and the foundation stones have the names of the twelve apostles. Entry to an eternal reward starts through Judaism but salvation itself rests on the church founded by Jesus Christ. The precious stones are similar to the list of precious stones in the vestment of the High Priest as given in Exodus 39:10-13, matching in nine of the stones.

The size of the building is 1,500 miles in length, breath and height. The area of the base of the building would be larger than half of the United States. Using the normal height of a story in a building, the 1,500 mile high city would produce about 880,000 stories. If each person were given even a square mile of floor space, the city would be adequate for nearly two trillion people. It would not seem that the dimensions of the building would be given in the visions but are selected by John to describe it. However, it is an immense structure and the description intends to more than fulfill Old Testament statements about Abraham's descendants being uncountable as does the number with white robes in this Book (6:9). Clearly the plan of God is to bring everyone to salvation and disciples are the primary witnesses to make that goal known. The destruction of the temple operations described earlier as Babylon might seem as an extreme reaction to the lack of a true witness to the covenant relationship. Yet, without witnesses, how can people make a clear choice. A lack of witnessing by disciples might produce a similar surprise for them as well. Whatever comes from God is for everyone and whoever hides revelation may not see it for themselves either (Ez 33:7-9). Christ came to show a union of human and divine life to the world; who could claim to live that life if it doesn't show as well?

CHAPTER 22 - Conclusion

The river of life comes in a never-ending stream from the throne of God to the city. The trees along it are trees of life. The whole sustenance of the city is the life of God and its very light. "They will reign for ever and ever" (22:5).

A series of instructions and clarifications close out the Book starting at 22:6. The message of the vision will be delivered by an angel which would be the Jewish understanding. The emphasis is on "soon" and the angel tells John "very soon I shall be with you again" (22:7) indicating the angel is coming. The "I, John" statement (22:8) would indicate that John was responsible for the entire writing between 1:9 and 22:15 even though some explanations in the text could have come from the time of the translation for clarification and the letters were added to introduce the entire vision to a Greek-speaking community. John kneeling at the feet of the angel to worship him and told not to do that since only God must be worshiped is repeated to tie the two celebration accounts together. Judaism kept the Law, a message brought by an angel, very loyally. They were awed by such great reverence for God that they shied away from direct use of the Divine Name. Now as the message is filled out with a living with God, in a sharing of God's life, the closeness to worship of the angel messenger must stop. Yet, this repetition of this event and what follows calls into question the identity of this "angel."

The final warning is "Do not keep the prophecies of the book a secret because the time is close" (22:10). The urgency of a coming that will occur raises the great question of the 19 centuries that have passed since this Book was written if the end of the first century is used to date it. Commentators suggest it is an apocalyptic metaphor, a misunderstanding by John, or that even a day for the Lord is like 1,000 years and 1,000 years like a day. Yet the writing is John's attempt to express a repeated meaning in the vision of a very short time to wait. The early context and Jesus' actual coming is much more appropriate.

Then after repeating the warning of the immediate coming, seemingly the angel refers to himself as "Alpha and Omega, the first and last, the beginning and the end." These terms have been used for "The Lord God" (1:8), the one who tells John to write (1:17), and "the One sitting on the throne" (21:6). The angel who has been speaking to John is equated with God and therefore is Jesus Christ, the one who brings the message to creation and also the king in heaven (Mt 25:31-34). Judaism, in worshiping the God who came to them, was always worshiping the son, Jesus Christ, before the incarnation (Jn 1:18). Their early worship even when condemned by the prophets was not false in their intention but in seeing God too much in the image of polytheism. When they switched to knowing only One God for all of creation, they worshiped the True God but could not carry out the full meaning of creation without the coming of Jesus Christ. Here the final message is played out by tieing God, Lamb and Jesus Christ together. The early context means the community of John the Evangelist would read these words and search the sayings of Jesus Christ to look for separate emphasis of this revelation. They found that connection and recorded his words in John's Gospel to show it was true. At that point, Christianity became complete and the initial message—the

Book of Revelation—also became fully understandable. John had heard the great message, the "seven thunderclaps." Was his worship before "the angel" false worship or only not allowed until the full message was known?

The closing of the message in the last six verses repeats the sending of the angel even though it is Jesus speaking. It is hard to imagine that the ending would be phrased in such a way if this were a Christian addition made after the Gospel of John the Evangelist. The statement that Jesus is "of David's line" or the "root of David" has only the meaning of Christian succession in proclaiming revelation at the end of the first century when all Christians have accepted Jesus as the Messiah and even used that as part of his name as Jesus Christ. Yet for John the Baptist, this would be the critical understanding for a prophecy on the coming of the Messiah delivered to his Jewish audience since it fulfilled the Old Testament prophecies. Jesus had to reassure John from the same source when John had questions while in prison (Mt 11:2-6). The Spirit and the bride (22:17) represent the Body of Christ—Holy Spirit and human (Jn 14:16-17)—and are the basis of the invitation to the world. Then comes the solemn warning about changing the message and far worse if not witnessing to all of it (22:18-19). The warning speaks to everyone who reads this Book or hears it proclaimed. To say this Book only promises a Messiah will come at some point in the future to rule on earth for "1,000 years," after the Divine Messiah has already come and brought the message in its fullness in the Gospel, is both an "addition" and a cutting out of the prophecies in this Book. To be silent about the full message is as dramatic a failure as a changing of it.

The one "who guarantees these revelations" must certainly be God since that is whose plan is presented here. The one who says he will "be with you soon," shown as an angel earlier (22:7), is Jesus Christ. The Book of Revelation as the opening to the New Testament period announces that the Messiah is one with God, truly Emmanuel (God with us) and the final Gospel writing confirms that in Jesus' own words. The final postscript in the New Testament to this Revelation tells us God is love and to live in love is to live God's life and, therefore, to live in God's love forever (1 Jn 4:16). From first to last—from this writing to the Gospel of John and his first letter—Revelation would be beyond belief in its greatness, except for the fact that it is guaranteed by God.

EPILOGUE

REVELATION AND THE FOURTH GOSPEL

An issue that should be raised in regard to the view of Revelation presented here is the connection between the Book of Revelation and John's Gospel. It is a very old tradition that Revelation came from the community responsible for the Gospel of John. Early arguments about that connection centered on the proposal that the author of the Gospel was responsible for Revelation as well. That question seems to have been answered in the negative by Dionysius, Bishop of Alexandria, (c. 250) even though the connection continued until the twentieth century at least in the title of Revelation in most bibles.

Some commentators on the Gospel of John see the Johannine community as somewhat separated from the apostolic church at an early time and returning to union only as Christianity becomes separated from Judaism. In the speculation that accompanies such a view, the community of John the Evangelist would be more open to fringe groups of Judaism or even to Gentiles. The fringe groups would include followers of John the Baptist, Essenes who accepted Christianity, Samaritans who accepted Christianity and the original Gentile Christians in Samaria. That would mean that such a community or set of churches could not be close to the apostolic church in Palestine which was not just united to Judaism but part of it.

The evidence of such relationships between the community of John the Evangelist and fringe groups is not substantial, but it is at least visible in the New Testament. John the son of Zebedee, if he is the Evangelist, was with Peter in bringing the Spirit (Confirmation) to the Samaritans, who were baptized by

Philip, one of the seven special disciples (Acts 8:14-17). That only indicates John was known to Philip's group. Cornelius, the Gentile baptized by Peter, was a resident in Samaria so he would surely be tied in to the Christian community of Philip at some point. Therefore, if John the son of Zebedee remained in contact with the church in Samaria, the Gentile Christians there also could be connected to him. John the son of Zebedee was probably one of the two disciples of John the Baptist who became disciples of Jesus (Jn 1:35-40); Andrew was the other. Any connection to Essenes would require the assumption that John the Baptist and his disciples had some relationship with the Essenes; a point not shown in the New Testament.

The execution of James the son of Zebedee by Herod Agrippa in 41-44 (Acts 12:1-5), the only time that Samaria was put under his control, indicates that James could have been involved with non-Jewish converts to Christianity. The execution "pleased the Jews" and Herod's persecution surely went beyond James as an individual. Peter was imprisoned and seemed destined for the same fate until he escaped from prison and apparently left Palestine. Those two events relating to apostles close to John the son of Zebedee would tend to indicate that John also was operating somewhat separate from Judaism, even though it hardly proves it.

The movement of John the son of Zebedee out of Palestine would follow the example of the remainder of the seven special disciples after Stephen was stoned (Acts 11:19). The tradition of John the Evangelist being in Ephesus and that the Fourth Gospel was written there would fit into such a move. Having been separated from Judaism early by activities in Samaria, John the Evangelist would be open to Gentile Christians elsewhere. The move might not have been directly to Ephesus so that Paul's presence in Ephesus, or traveling through Samaria on journeys to Jerusalem, could be recorded without a mention of John the son of Zebedee. However, the initial work on John's views for justifying a separation from Judaism may have been incorporated into writings at such an early time and used later as a basis for John's Gospel.

Christianity underwent a great change from the initial post-Resurrection community to the separation from Judaism after the destruction of the temple in 70. What had been a Jewish sect that accepted Jesus as the Jewish Messiah and waited for Him to return and set up a kingdom, opened itself to Gentiles and then by degrees moved away from the Law until it finally became completely separated from Judaism after 70. The community of John the Evangelist would have made the same journey in a much quicker fashion if it became open to Samaritan and Gentile converts earlier as might be seen in Acts in the first decade after the Resurrection. Jewish Christians would have found such a shift difficult to accept even while remaining Christian with its promise of salvation. Gentile Christians who were Godfearers when baptized would have questioned that change, and both Matthew's and Luke's Gospels seem to relate to such questions by each of those groups.

The destruction of the temple in 70 would have brought everything into question in the same way Judaism began an internal questioning of themselves when they suffered the Exile in Babylon after the earlier temple was destroyed. Some commentators search in the New Testament writings for evidence of knowledge relating to the temple being destroyed since such a major event could hardly be ignored. The letter to the Hebrews could be seen as a writing which addressed that problem even though the destruction is not mentioned in it.

The availability of the Book of Revelation, if it were a writing that described a vision of the plan of God witnessed by John the Baptist before Jesus' public life, could have provided a proper answer. In that case, the destruction of the temple and Jerusalem would have been foretold before the message of the Messiah was proclaimed. Such knowledge would mean that Christianity had not lost its way in separating from temple-oriented Judaism and did so in response to the command to "Come out, my people, away from her, so you do not share in her crimes and have the same plagues to bear" (18:4). The community of John the Evangelist would recognize the event as a validation of their Christian journey. If John the Baptist's disciples, present in

Ephesus (Acts 19:1-7), brought this writing with them to John the Evangelist, it would have been welcomed. More likely is that they would have brought it earlier and the coming doom of Jerusalem would have been foreseen shortly after the Jewish revolt started in 66. The Christian communities left Jewish Palestine for Pella near the start of the revolt which indicates they didn't expect divine protection for Jerusalem.

Revelation, studied in relation to such a situation by the community of John the Evangelist, would have suggested something even greater about the whole meaning of Christianity. The post-Resurrection church view of an early second coming to establish a kingdom would have been erased through a reading of Revelation by the church. Revelation shows a coming of Jesus at the time of the crucifixion and then "1,000 years" later at the judgment.

A far more important aspect of reading Revelation would be the dramatic closeness of Jesus, as the Lamb, to the heavenly throne and his role in opening the plan of God. There is a shift of worship to the Lamb by creation (four animals) and by the fullness of heavenly Israel (24 elders) (5:7-10). Such an occurrence in heaven carries a divinity meaning in very clear terms. The double recording of John in Revelation kneeling to worship an "angel" indicates that John also must have thought there was a closeness to Divinity than would be expected from an earthly messiah. Then the response of the "angel" at the end of the vision (22:13), using the titles that reflected God in the second introduction (1:8), provides the divinity indications. Even if the introductions and the ending were not included in the first draft of Revelation that might have been shown to the community of John the Evangelist, the language (22:13) still carries an unexpected connection to divinity.

The community of John the Evangelist would look at the words of Jesus collected from his public life for evidence of a divine statement, especially if it were clear that Revelation were a writing that preceded the public life of Jesus. To have only a later writing, not tied directly to Jesus, that added a proclamation of Jesus as divine might have been considered blasphemy and rejected. John the Evangelist, if John the son of Zebedee, might recognize some claims of Jesus that could be interpreted as supporting a divinity statement. They would become more clear after reading the Revelation account than such statements might have been during Jesus' public life.

The divinity statements of Jesus used in the Gospel of John are tied to Jesus applying the Divine Name from the Old Testament, "Yahweh" or "I Am," to himself. When Jesus actually made such statements the words would have been spoken in Aramaic. Such a use could have raised a suspicion even though Jesus' words would not have been exactly the same as the Hebrew "Yahweh" nor "I Am" nor fit exactly with the explanation of "I Am" in Exodus 3:14. Only after moving to Ephesus, and being involved with Greek-speaking Gentile Christians and the Greek Septuagint for a text, would the Greek translation of Jesus' words for I Am—Ego Eimi—be seen as exactly the same as the Greek version of "I Am" in Exodus 3:14.

Only when the hint of Jesus as the incarnation of God had been raised, and at least considered seriously, could the words of Jesus in his public life be investigated for such a message. One could theorize that such a concept simply crept into the mind of John the Evangelist over time, or that a disciple accidentally noticed the sameness between Jesus' claim and the explanation of the Divine Name in Exodus. However, it seems quite possible that the reading of a Greek translation of an Aramaic recording of the vision introducing the prophecy about the coming of the Messiah by a disciple provided the impetus to examine the connection further. If a disciple, who had been with Jesus in his public life, was available for consultation that person would be told of the coincidence between the parallel uses of Ego Eimi and then the need for the last Gospel would be recognized.

Revelation would be important to the community of John the Evangelist and an important and lasting association would be guaranteed. The Book would be recognized as exceedingly important to the Christian church and be quoted often over the next century. Revelation, with its explanation of the whole plan of God, would hardly be ignored. Only later, as the Gospel of John carried the full meaning, would Revelation become less dominant and, as the church moved more fully into the Gentile Greek culture, would a writing with such a Jewish orientation and the Aramaic thinking pattern be less used. The argument that the author of John's Gospel could not be the same John as the author of Revelation raised questions about the acceptability of Revelation as a writing to be included into the New Testament canon in the Eastern Church. Accepting the argument and looking for another John as the author of the Book of Revelation opens the writing to a new appreciation.

Two sections in John's Gospel, in addition to the John the Baptist sections, indicate a closeness to Revelation. The first of these is the cleansing of the temple scene (Jn 2:13-22) which is set early in Jesus' public life. It is on an early trip to Jerusalem while John the Baptist is still free to baptize. The action of Jesus is directed more at the animals used for sacrifices at the temple than in the other Gospels where the same scene is tied to Jeremiah 7 in the "robbers den" comment. There the emphasis is on the failure of the Jewish leaders to identify the Messiah for the nation so any connection to Revelation is lost. In John the comment "stop turning my Father's house into a market" focuses directly on the animals. The abandonment of the temple worship by God in Revelation (17:17) while at the same time calling the people "away from her" could relate to the continuation of animal sacrifices, common to pagan views of worshiping gods. When the Jewish view of only One God for all of creation became known, the meaning of sacrifices as the worship of that God should have been addressed.

The second section related to temple worship in John's Gospel is the statement of Jesus to the woman at the well (4:21-24). The magnitude of the change in worship, its direction against temple sacrifices, and its closeness as "here already" suggests the temple destruction shown in Revelation. The quotation gives the same emphasis that seems to come from the conclusion that with a change in relationship with God, the acts of worship would also change. That conclusion would tie closely to

John the Baptist's anger at Pharisees and Sadducees coming for baptism (Mt 3:7-12).

A change in Christian understanding occurs during the first century which can be seen in a comparison of Revelation as the understanding of the vision at the start and the picture in the Gospel of John and the First Letter of John at the end. The picture in Revelation uses terms such as "the anger of the Lamb" (6:16), a flow of blood from "the winepress of God's anger" (14:19), and "the wine of Almighty God's fierce anger" (19:16). It also presents an image of a terrible battle where the Messiah kills a great many opponents (19:18).

The Gospel emphasizes God's love for the world where believing brings eternal life and condemnation comes from not believing with hardly a mention of judgment and none of violence (Jn 3:16-19). The heart of the Gospel message is in a solemn warning that "eating the flesh of the Son of Man and drinking His blood" (Jn 6:53)—putting on the life of Christ—are all that is required for eternal life. Great signs are given to show that belief in Jesus is most certainly supported by God so no one should fail to accept eternal life. The letter, interpreting the Gospel, promises that "God is love and anyone who lives in love lives in God and God lives in Him" (1 Jn 4:16).

Salvation comes as creation disappears without a hint of a battle and with only the terror of realization by those who have failed to grasp the need to put on Christ. The language of the Old Testament can be used to tell the Old Testament people how the early revelation will be fulfilled since they wouldn't listen to any other language. Yet, the full meaning can only be realized in the words of Jesus spoken to the whole world and applying to all human life of all time.

The Book of Revelation appears to be a bridge between the Old Testament revelation and the coming of a Divine Messiah who completes the whole revelation for the whole of humanity. When it is read with that point of view in mind, the small message about a supposed persecution near the end of the first century disappears and the greatest message of all time is introduced.

128

END NOTES

1.	Pontifical Biblical Commission, <u>The Interpretation of the Bible in the Church</u>, (Boston: St. Paul Books and Media, 1993)
2.	Adela Yarbo Collins, <u>Reading the Book of Revelation in the Twentieth Century</u>, Interpretation (1986) p. 236
3.	Raymond E. Brown and John P. Meier, <u>Antioch and Rome</u>, (New York: Paulist Press 1983) p. 48
4.	J. Massyngberde Ford, <u>Revelation</u> - Anchor Bible, (Garden City, NY: Doubleday 1980) pg. 37
5.	IBID., p. 30-33
6.	IBID., p. 38
7.	IBID., p. 39-41
8.	IBID., p. 56
9.	Eugenio Corsini, <u>The Apocalypse—The Perennial Revelation of Jesus Christ</u>, (Wilmington, Del: Michael Glazier Inc. 1983)
10.	Ford, op. cit., p. 50
11.	IBID., p. 46
12.	IBID., p. 48
13.	IBID., p. 12
14.	Duane F. Watson, <u>Anchor Bible Dictionary</u>, (New York: Doubleday 1992) Vol. 4, p. 1107
15.	IBID., p. 71
16.	<u>New American Bible</u>, (New York: Catholic Book Publishing Co. 1991)